IDIOT'S GUIDES.
AS EASY AS IT GETS!

Puppies

by Connie Swaim and Deb M. Eldredge, DVM

ALPHA

A member of Penguin Random House LLC

ALPHA BOOKS

Published by Penguin Random House LLC

Penguin Random House LLC, 345 Hudson Street, New York, New York 10014, USA • Penguin Random House (Canada), 320 Front Street West, Suite 1400, Toronto, Ontario M5V 3B6, Canada • Penguin Books Ltd., 80 Strand, London WC2R 0RL, England • Penguin Ireland, 25 St. Stephen's Green, Dublin 2, Ireland (a division of Penguin Books Ltd.) • Penguin Random House (Australia), 707 Collins St, Docklands, Victoria 3008, Australia • Penguin Books India Pvt. Ltd., 3rd Floor Mindmill Corporate Tower, Plot No. 24A, Sector 16A, Film City, Noida, UP 201 301, India • Penguin Random House LLC (NZ), 67 Apollo Drive, Rosedale, North Shore, Auckland 1311, New Zealand (a division of Pearson New Zealand Ltd.) • Penguin Books (South Africa) (Pty.) Ltd., 24 Sturdee Avenue, Rosebank, Johannesburg 2196, South Africa • Penguin Books Ltd., Registered Offices: 80 Strand, London WC2R 0RL, England

003-265612-December2014

International Standard Book Number: 978-1-61564-645-6

Library of Congress Catalog Card Number: 2014941124

18 17 16   9 8 7 6 5 4 3

Interpretation of the printing code: The rightmost number of the first series of numbers is the year of the book's printing; the rightmost number of the second series of numbers is the number of the book's printing. For example, a printing code of 14-1 shows that the first printing occurred in 2014.

Printed in China

Publisher: **Mike Sanders**
Executive Managing Editor: **Billy Fields**
Executive Acquisitions Editor: **Lori Cates Hand**
Development Editor: **John Etchison**
Production Editor: **Jana M. Stefanciosa**

Design Supervisor: **William Thomas**
Photography: **Katherine Scheele**
Layout: **Ayanna Lacey**
Indexer: **Heather McNeill**
Proofreader: **Laura Caddell**

Contents

Introduction

Bringing a puppy into your life is a time of great joy. Ensuring the puppy will become a wonderful companion for the rest of its life will take time and dedication on your part. Breeding, early socialization, and temperament all play some part in what your dog will become when it grows up. However, you will be the most important component in determining how your puppy behaves as it matures. Many of the problems people have with their dogs can be traced to inconsistent training or incorrect training practices.

This book will guide you on the path to getting the most out of life for both you and your puppy. If you haven't gotten a puppy yet, the book will help you choose the one most suited for your lifestyle. If you already have a puppy, the book will help with such important matters as housebreaking, training good behavior, and solving issues between children and puppies. Nutrition, grooming, and veterinary relationships are also extremely important to your puppy's well-being. Our veterinarian will help you navigate the often confusing byways of food and health care.

Most of all, we want this book to help you so your puppy never becomes a statistic. According to the American Society for the Prevention of Cruelty to Animals, millions of dogs are taken to animal shelters or re-homed each year. Often it is a behavioral issue that causes the original owner to no longer want to care for his or her pet. A puppy should be a lifelong commitment. This book will keep you on the right path to making your home the puppy's forever home.

Thank You

Connie Swaim: I would like to thank my husband, Curtis Robb, for his patience while the writing of this book took over my life. Special thanks to Patrick M. Leer, who read every word and offered valuable suggestions, and to Laura VanArendonk Baugh for introducing me to clicker training.

Dr. Eldredge: I would like to thank the many puppies who have been a part of my life—both as clients and as my own personal pets. Puppies are a special gift of love and companionship. Special thanks to my very understanding current dogs who put up with me working instead of playing with them nonstop: 15-year-old Ms Dani and two-year-olds Babe and Doc.

Special thanks to the following who shared their puppies or their homes and businesses for the photos used in this book: Humane Society of Indianapolis; Platinum Paws Grooming Salon, Carmel, Indiana; Alena VanArendonk; Melissa Heigl and her wonderful children; Nyle Miller (Ranger); Natosha Cook (Luna); Barb Beland (Kesh); Patsy Scott (Glamour Girl On The Ride); Laura Baugh (Mindy); Michelle Smit (Zoey); Elizabeth Wysong (Lucy); Bill Ipsen (Smash); Danielle May (Duke); Robyn Ritter (Kindle); Laura Baker (Niles); Beth Lines (Cricket); Carrie Douglas (Annie); Danette Lerner (Lucy); Cheryl Troyer (Marley); Tracy Gritter (Tilly); Elizabeth Wyatt (Cody); Amber Tatom (Moses); and Heather Foster (Lulu Belle).

Chapter 1
Choosing a Puppy

- Making sure your house, home, and family are ready for a puppy
- Finding and choosing the best puppy for you

There is just something about a puppy that makes our hearts melt. Even people who don't like dogs will generally stop and smile when they see a puppy. But getting a puppy should be something you do with your head and not your melting heart.

Often the purchase or adoption of a puppy is a snap decision based on falling in love with that cute puppy face. You pick up the puppy, it licks your ear or face, and that's it: you fall in love and take it home. Then you discover you got something with extremely sharp teeth that has no regard for where it goes to the bathroom and what it chews up. Knowing what you are getting into and thinking it through will ensure that you get a puppy that is right for your life.

Besides impulse, there are various other reasons people choose puppies. Some people get a puppy because they want to do something specific with it, such as a sport or therapy work. Many parents get puppies because their kids just have to have one.

Make sure you are getting your puppy for the right reasons, and that you have the time to devote to it. Remember, the puppy will be with you for years—often remaining long after the children who begged for it have left for college.

When you are looking at litters of puppies, it's very easy to want them all. However, it's better to get only one puppy at a time. Some puppies that grow up with littermates will bond with the littermates more than with their humans. And if you get two puppies at the same time, it can be difficult to devote enough time to both of them. Two puppies are twice the work. If you want a second dog, wait three to five months before you decide to add that next canine family member.

Are You Ready for a New Family Member?

Before you get a puppy, make sure you really want a dog for the long term. Many dogs, including purebreds, end up in animal shelters or on classified lists once they hit 6 to 8 months old. It's no longer the cute, fluffy thing you fell in love with but is instead an adolescent with adolescent issues. No matter what your children promise you, most parents end up being the ones who care for the puppy. Some parents get the dog in an effort to teach children responsibility, but if your children don't take it seriously, make sure the puppy doesn't suffer the consequences. The puppy should be your responsibility for life, no matter what happens.

Kids and Puppies

If you have children under the age of 10, you must be prepared to always supervise interactions between the child and puppy. Many dog bites to children happen when the child and puppy are left unsupervised.

Children may trap a puppy in a corner or pull its tail. This could cause the puppy to be afraid of children, or worse, to become aggressive or start growling at children. Don't allow young children to pick puppies up and carry them around. This can be very stressful for the pup. Also, teach kids not to allow the puppy to lick them on the face. It is estimated that 77 percent of dog bites to children are on the face.

Keep Your Puppy Indoors

Dogs are social creatures. They need a lot of time with family members. Do not get a puppy if she can't be a part of your family. Dogs left outside all of the time, especially dogs that are tied up, may have more behavioral issues and be more likely to bite than dogs that live with their humans. Most outdoor dogs spend their time at the back door wanting in. Or they become bored and dig up the yard or become escape artists. Your dog needs to be primarily a house pet.

All puppies are going to be extremely active and need walks and playtime, but some breeds remain more active and require more exercise as adults. For example, most Jack Russell terriers or any herding breeds will need space to run all their lives, as well as an owner dedicated to making playtime fun. There are some small dogs that were bred just to be lap dogs, such as the Maltese or Pekinese. These breeds are often suited to a more sedentary life. Before you get a puppy, consider what you want from a companion that may live 10 to 15 years or more.

Size and Breed

Don't choose a dog based on size alone. Many people who have apartments or small homes choose a small breed, thinking it won't need much space. But many terrier breeds need room to run, as they were originally bred to hunt. Some of the giant breeds such as the Irish Wolfhound don't require a lot of exercise, especially once they're past the puppy stage.

If you have fallen in love with a certain breed, go to the library or online and research that breed before you get a dog. If you buy from a responsible breeder, the breeder will be able to provide information on the dog's energy level as it grows up, what its temperament around children might be, and so on. If you are buying a dog from someone who can't answer those types of questions, move on to a different breeder. However, breed guidelines are just that: guidelines. Individual dogs will vary. Much about how the dog turns out will be the result of the work you put into it.

Consider the Cost

Think about what it will cost to take care of your pet. At the bare minimum, your dog will require a yearly visit to the veterinarian. Your puppy will need food, a collar and leash, bedding, a crate, toys, and things to chew on. Some breeds such as English Bulldogs are also prone to serious health issues. Even a mixed-breed dog could have health issues that may not show up until the dog is older. The bottom line is your pet will cost money, and nothing is more devastating than to have to relinquish a beloved companion due to the inability to pay for treatment for a serious medical issue.

Do You Need a Fenced Yard?

If you just can't imagine getting up at 5 A.M. to walk the dog before you go to work, rain or shine, warm or cold, then you will need a fenced yard. However, dogs do require physical interaction with their people. So even if you have a fenced yard, your dog will need you to play with him.

Some people imagine the dog will be happier running free outside than being crated or confined in a home. However, dogs left alone outdoors tend to become very frantic when their owners come outside. This may lead to the owner coming out less and the dog becoming more stressed. Your dog should never be just an outside dog. If you can't interact with your dog for several hours every day, then it may not be a good idea to have a dog.

Socialization

Dogs require socialization, meaning you will need to take your puppy to new places and to meet new people. A serious issue many owners face is a puppy that grows into an adult dog that growls at strangers who visit. Puppies that are isolated from an early age or are left in a backyard without adequate human interaction may grow into adult dogs that have issues with strangers.

Some Breeds Need More Grooming

Some dogs shed more than others. For example, German Shepherds shed their coats at least twice a year. During this time, the undercoat comes out in huge chunks and it is easy to have a house full of flying fur. There are dogs that will need regular grooming all their lives to keep their coats looking good. Poodles need regular trips to the groomer in order to keep that perfect poodle look. Consider the time you will spend cleaning up fur or the time and money spent at a groomer.

If you have the time and resources, a puppy will be an amazing addition to your family. She will provide a lifetime of love and companionship. Just make sure your lifestyle and your wallet can handle the new addition.

Evaluate Your Home

If you own your own home, there will be fewer things to be concerned about when you are ready to get a puppy. However, if you rent your home or apartment, you should check with your landlord or rental company prior to getting a puppy. Some rental agencies have breed or size restrictions. Even your insurance company could have restrictions on what breeds you can own. Many apartments also restrict the number of animals you can keep. Check your city or county ordinances to see if there are breed restrictions or if there is a limit to how many pets a homeowner can have.

Fences

Does your neighborhood have any restrictions on the type of fence you can have, or how high it can be? Some areas won't allow homeowners to put up fences. Invisible fences can be an option, but consult with a trainer and do some research before you decide if this is a good route for you.

If you have a guarding breed like a German Shepherd or a hound such as a Beagle, a privacy fence might be a good option. Many homeowners are faced with nuisance complaints due to barking dogs. Often a fence that prevents the dog from seeing what is on the other side will help with this issue. If you have a Border Collie or other extremely athletic dog that could easily clear a standard 4-foot fence, consider putting in a 6-foot fence instead.

A Challenge to Keep Clean

No matter how diligent you are, your puppy will at one time or another pee or poop in your home. It may tear up furniture or scratch the doors. Even breeds that are purported to not shed will still lose some fur, and some breeds shed a lot. And when it's wet outside, your puppy will track in mud. Keep in mind you are getting an animal and it won't be perfect.

Some dogs do shed less than others. Many terriers as well as Maltese and Lhasa Apsos are breeds that don't shed much. There are numerous online resources that provide lists of dogs that are light shedders.

Choose the Right Puppy

Now that you've done your research and thought about the financial and lifestyle changes a puppy will bring, it's time for the fun part: picking out your puppy!

The Right Age to Bring Home a Puppy

It is always better for the social and mental development of pups if they can stay with their mom and littermates until at least 8 weeks. Puppies taken away from their litter too early may have more issues in terms of learning to share resources and learning not to bite (also known as *bite inhibition*). If your puppy is less than 8 weeks of age, immediately consult with a trainer who specializes in puppy training to get your pup into social groups with other puppies as soon as possible.

Observing the Litter

One of the best ways to pick a puppy is to observe pups when they are with their littermates. Obviously, this is not always possible, but if you get the opportunity it may make it easier to pick a puppy that will be a perfect fit for your home.

Good with Kids

If you have children under the age of 10, it may be best to choose a puppy that is not too shy or too boisterous. A puppy that is too shy may need extra work on socialization and could have fear issues that could lead to biting. A puppy that is too boisterous may be constantly jumping on children.

Both the too-shy puppy and the over-the-top puppy will probably require an experienced dog owner who is willing to do extra work and get into training classes immediately.

Meeting the Puppy

1

If at all possible, you should sit quietly in a large room with the puppy you are considering and see what happens. Look for a puppy that is willing to come and say hello to you without you coaxing it. See how the puppy acts with her siblings. You want a puppy that is playful and can both jump on the back of her sibling and let the sibling jump on her back so there is give and take in the play. If your family includes children, bring the kids with you to choose the puppy. You need to know that a squealing 3-year-old won't frighten the puppy too much.

2

Allow the puppies to explore you and see what happens if they nip your hand. If they begin nipping your hand with some pressure, give a high-pitched squeal or say "ouch!" and immediately stop and turn your head away from the puppy. A puppy that stops nipping and backs off for a moment may be easier to teach bite inhibition. Give the puppy a few chances to learn that your squeal and stopping the interaction are the result of her biting your hand.

The number-one thing to consider when choosing a puppy is to not let your emotions rule your choice. It's human nature to want to take the most pathetic one, or the one that appears to need us the most. People especially seem drawn to puppies that appear overly shy or nervous. But choosing a confident puppy that is interested in interacting with you and appears healthy and alert is almost always the best idea, especially for first-time pet owners or families that include children.

Gently pick up the puppy and see how she reacts. A puppy that struggles excessively and bites may not be a good choice, especially in a family with children. You don't want to squeeze the puppy, and don't frighten it by flipping it on its back. Immediately put the puppy down and see what happens. Does it stay around to interact with you more, or does it run and hide? You want a puppy confident enough to decide that playing with you is interesting, not scary.

Make some low-level noises such as jingling your car keys or squeezing an empty plastic water bottle. How does the puppy react to the noise? You want a puppy that reacts but is able to recover when it figures out the noise isn't threatening. If the puppy runs away and starts shaking or won't come back out again even when the noise is gone, the puppy may lack confidence.

Take a good look at the puppy. Do you notice any physical defects? You want a puppy that appears alert and has some fat over his ribs. Look especially at the nose and eyes. If the puppy has discharge around either the nose or the eyes, consult with your veterinarian before taking him. If he isn't moving much or appears listless, he may not be the puppy for you.

Where to Find Puppies

Finding a puppy is easy. You can find them offered for free in classified ads, or you can pay thousands of dollars for one from a top-notch breeder. Deciding which course of action is the best for you is the hard part.

Whatever route you take, just remember the old adage that there is no such thing as a "free" puppy. Even if you get a puppy that doesn't cost anything to acquire, the pup will still cost plenty in terms of lifelong care.

Animal Shelters and Rescue Groups

Animal shelters are great places to find puppies. Not only are you saving a life, but many shelters spay or neuter the puppy prior to adoption and may provide first shots and implant a microchip for identification as part of the adoption package. Often the adoption fee is far less than the cost would have been had you paid to have all the work done yourself. And if you just have to have a purebred puppy, about 25 percent of animals in shelters are purebred.

There are also many breed-specific rescues that may have puppies for people looking for a specific breed. Just do an internet search for your favorite breed and the word "rescue," and see whether there is a nearby rescue organization for that breed. Then contact them about the availability of puppies.

Many shelters and rescue groups also do some behavior evaluation on the puppies and may be able to tell you whether the puppy will be a good fit for a family with young children, or if the puppy would do better in an extremely active, adult-only home.

Breeders

Breeders are people who deliberately mate dogs to produce a litter of puppies. There are many fantastic breeders in the world who spend hours researching both the male and female dog's medical and behavioral history before deciding which dogs should be bred together. Other breeders just breed to produce a litter of puppies and hope to make a little money by cashing in on whatever breed or mix of breeds is popular at the time.

Pick a purebred puppy based on the integrity of the breeder. It's best to buy from a person who allows you to meet the mother of the puppies. If you can meet the father, too, that's even better. The parents should be friendly and well cared for. While some of a dog's temperament is influenced by how it is raised, a lot is also influenced by the temperament of the parents, which is why it is always a good idea to meet them.

If you are picking a breed known for a particular health issue, ask the breeder what testing has been done to minimize the possibility that the puppies carry such defects.

Ask your breeder if he or she has a return policy. Many reputable breeders stand behind their puppies and will take them back if temperament or health issues arise. Most importantly, find a breeder who asks you questions and works to find the puppy in the litter that is best suited for you instead of a breeder who only cares if you can pay the puppy's asking price. Ask for references of people who have purchased from this breeder in the past and then call them to see how the pups turned out. You want to know if the dogs are medically sound and if they are good family pets.

If you are buying from a breeder, you may also be able to visit the puppies a few times before you pick one. Watching how they mature will also help you make a decision about which one may be best for your family.

A good breeder will also be able to help you with the puppy for the rest of its life. Breeders should be able to recommend food, grooming, and medical information that is specific to the breed you are purchasing. If the breeder appears to not know that much about the breed or dog you are getting, choose another breeder.

Pet Stores and Online

Buying a puppy from a pet store can be controversial. However, some pet stores offer puppies from local animal shelters. While there may be pet shops that sell only puppies from quality breeders, many stores sell dogs that come from puppy mills. According to the ASPCA, "A puppy mill is a large-scale commercial dog breeding operation that places profit over the well-being of its dogs—who are often severely neglected—and acts without regard to responsible breeding practices."

Many puppies offered online may also be from puppy mills. If you are buying a puppy in a pet shop or online, ask for the name of the breeder and contact that person. Find out if visiting the parents of the puppy is possible. Most sellers of puppy mill puppies won't be able to provide a means to visit the parents. Research the kennel name and find out how many puppies they produce per year. If the person you research has many different breeds listed and is producing hundreds of puppies a year, that is a puppy mill. Do your homework before buying the puppy to ensure that your puppy came from a reputable source.

Puppies from puppy mills are often more difficult to housebreak than other puppies because they are never let out of their cages. They may have more health problems because there is no regard paid to what health issues the parents may have. The breeders are just producing whatever is popular as quickly as possible.

However, what most people consider the real tragedy of puppy mills is the treatment of the parents of the puppies. They spend their entire lives in cramped conditions producing puppies without benefit of human contact. By buying a puppy from a puppy mill you are condemning the parents to producing another litter.

Chapter 2

Preparing for Your Puppy

- Making your house and yard safe for a puppy
- Buying crates, bowls, leashes, collars, and toys
- Preparing family members and other pets

You've done your research, you know how much work the puppy is going to take, and you have decided the time is right to bring the little guy or girl into your life. Now what? There is a lot to do to get ready for the puppy and ensure that your first weeks together are fun rather than frazzled.

Your puppy is going to require quite a bit of time, especially in those first few months as you get to know each other. Don't get a puppy if you are about to leave for a vacation, or during a time when you will be especially busy. If you are getting the puppy as a gift for your family during the holidays, consider getting her well before or after the big day to maximize the time you will be able to spend with the pup.

The first few weeks are generally the most expensive, as you buy everything you need. If money is tight, plan ahead and begin buying a few items at a time. If you have plenty of time to prepare, then you can also look at classified ads for gently used items that might help stretch your budget.

Decide where your puppy will eat and sleep before you bring her home. She should have a place away from children and other pets for both eating and sleeping. Invest in baby gates or exercise pens to help keep your puppy where you want her to be.

Setting a Budget

Even a free puppy is going to require some startup money. She will require shots, flea control, and heartworm-prevention medications. You will need to buy food, equipment, and toys. If your puppy didn't come spayed or neutered, you should factor that into your budget as well.

Puppies are notorious chewers, and many of the best chewing options are expensive. Look at the cost of bully sticks, elk antlers, and hollow rubber feeding toys to help figure out what you will need to spend on a monthly basis.

For the cost conscious, see if your area offers low-cost vaccine clinics or low-cost spay and neuter clinics. These clinics should never replace a veterinarian, but they may be an option if you need to save money. Your puppy should still be examined by a veterinarian as soon as possible after bringing him home, and he will require at least a yearly trip to the vet for a health checkup.

Depending on what shots your puppy got while with a breeder or at a shelter, he may still need one or two trips to the vet or vaccine clinic about a month apart.

If you haven't owned a dog in a while, call around to a few veterinary offices to inquire about the costs of wellness visits, shots, and spaying and neutering. If you are looking for low-cost options, check with local dog rescues or animal shelters.

Checklist

- Collars and leashes
  $20 to $75 depending on quality
- Crate
  $50 to $150 depending on size and type
- Chewing options
  $50 to $100 a month depending on the size of your puppy
- Heartworm and flea preventative
  $25 to $50 a month depending on the puppy's size
- Microchip
  $10 to $60
- Food
  $50 to $100 a month depending on the quality of food and size of the puppy

- Toys
  $50 to infinity depending on how quickly your puppy chews up the toys
- Bedding
  $30 to $75 depending on the size of the puppy
- Cleanup products for housebreaking mistakes
  $30 a month until your puppy is housebroken
- First shots
  $35 to $250 depending on what you get and whether it is at a low-cost clinic or a veterinarian's office; $35 to $100 annually after that

Puppy Proofing Your House

Puppies explore their world through their mouths. This means they are going to chew just about anything they can get their mouths on.

Go about puppy proofing your home in the same way you would if you were bringing home a young child. Look at your home from the level of the puppy. What can he reach? What cabinet doors could he pull open? Products commonly found under sinks, in laundry rooms, and in the garage are often hazardous to dogs, so make sure your puppy can't get into cleaners, antifreeze, and similar items.

Power Cords

There's something about power cords that appeals to many puppies. One woman had a puppy chew through four power cords to her laptop in a week, at a cost of about $80 per cord. Another woman who took her puppy to her office for a morning of socialization heard a yelp and came back to her office to find the puppy with burn marks on its tongue and mouth after it had chewed through a cord. The puppy had been left alone for less than five minutes.

Consider spraying your power cords with a deterrent. Many pet stores sell products designed to taste bad to puppies, which can be sprayed on anything you do not want the puppy to chew. However, there are some puppies who even find the taste of the deterrent appealing. Always be vigilant and don't rely on a deterrent to keep the puppy away from trouble.

Toys and Clothing

Children's toys and clothing are another hazard. Puppies (and many older dogs) seem to have an affinity for certain items of clothing, with socks and undergarments at the top of the list. Swallowing a sock could be life threatening and require surgery. Many a child's toy has been lost to sharp puppy teeth. Children will need to understand that the puppy will not know the difference between his toys and their toys. The puppy doesn't understand sharing.

Trash Containers

Be sure your trash containers either are in a cabinet or have a lid that would be difficult for a puppy to remove. Trash can smell really awesome to a pup, and some of the things he might pull out of the trash could cause tummy upset. Don't forget the bathroom trash as well.

Rugs and Flooring

If you have rugs, carpeting, or wood floors that would be especially difficult to clean, block off those rooms until the puppy is reliably housebroken. Chances are very good that your puppy will have accidents, so restrict him to areas where cleaning will be easiest.

The bottom line is if there is something in your home that your puppy can reach and you don't want him to have his teeth on it, put it away until he outgrows the need to chew up everything he can find. Keep your puppy near you at all times to ensure he doesn't get into mischief. A good rule of thumb: if it is too quiet and you can't see your puppy, he probably has gotten into something he shouldn't!

Puppy Proofing Your Yard

If your yard is fenced, an obvious first step is to carefully inspect the fence to make sure there are no puppy-size holes. Carefully monitor your puppy during his first weeks in your yard to see if he tests the fence or tries to dig under it. Puppies are amazingly resourceful when it comes to finding their way out of things.

Avoiding Damage to Your Yard

Check your yard for objects your puppy could destroy, such as hoses, lawn sprinklers, decorative fencing around flowers, and so on. Puppies love to dig, and it is difficult to teach them what is the yard and what is your prized flower bed. If you have flowers or shrubbery that could be easily damaged by a playful puppy, consider putting up a fence around those items until your puppy is older.

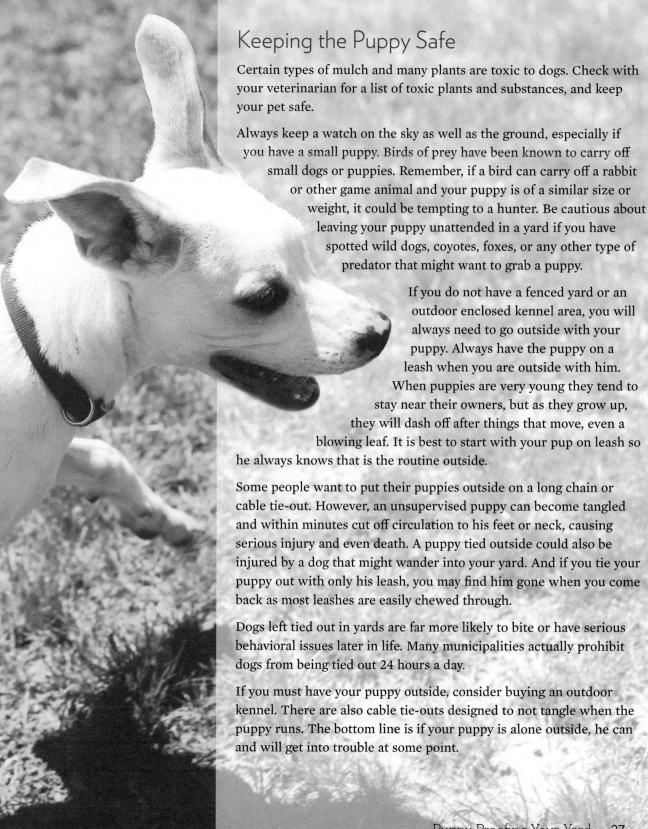

Keeping the Puppy Safe

Certain types of mulch and many plants are toxic to dogs. Check with your veterinarian for a list of toxic plants and substances, and keep your pet safe.

Always keep a watch on the sky as well as the ground, especially if you have a small puppy. Birds of prey have been known to carry off small dogs or puppies. Remember, if a bird can carry off a rabbit or other game animal and your puppy is of a similar size or weight, it could be tempting to a hunter. Be cautious about leaving your puppy unattended in a yard if you have spotted wild dogs, coyotes, foxes, or any other type of predator that might want to grab a puppy.

If you do not have a fenced yard or an outdoor enclosed kennel area, you will always need to go outside with your puppy. Always have the puppy on a leash when you are outside with him. When puppies are very young they tend to stay near their owners, but as they grow up, they will dash off after things that move, even a blowing leaf. It is best to start with your pup on leash so he always knows that is the routine outside.

Some people want to put their puppies outside on a long chain or cable tie-out. However, an unsupervised puppy can become tangled and within minutes cut off circulation to his feet or neck, causing serious injury and even death. A puppy tied outside could also be injured by a dog that might wander into your yard. And if you tie your puppy out with only his leash, you may find him gone when you come back as most leashes are easily chewed through.

Dogs left tied out in yards are far more likely to bite or have serious behavioral issues later in life. Many municipalities actually prohibit dogs from being tied out 24 hours a day.

If you must have your puppy outside, consider buying an outdoor kennel. There are also cable tie-outs designed to not tangle when the puppy runs. The bottom line is if your puppy is alone outside, he can and will get into trouble at some point.

What to Buy Before the Puppy Comes Home

It helps to have some of the basics before you bring the puppy home. Remember, puppies grow up fast. If you want your dog to have designer outfits, collars, and leashes, wait until your pup is close to its adult size to buy them. As your puppy grows it will be especially important to make sure his collar, crate, bedding, and toys are the appropriate size. A ball that might be perfect for a 2-month-old puppy could become a choking hazard for a 5-month-old.

A Crate

A crate is going to be one of your most important purchases. There are several different types of crates, but the important part is that it must be large enough for the puppy to be comfortable, but small enough so he won't have room to pee or poop. Dogs don't like to sleep where they pee, so the crate would have to be small enough so he would have to lay in pee if he had an accident. Once the puppy is housebroken, the crate can be larger. If you want to save money, you should look for a crate that comes with a divider. This type of crate will enable you to have a crate large enough to fit your puppy after she grows up, but that can be made smaller for when she first comes home.

Bedding

The type of bedding you choose may depend a lot on the breed of puppy you have. Long-coated, cold-weather breeds such as Huskies may just want to lie on the cold floor rather than curl up in a blanket. On the other hand, a Chihuahua may want a bed in which he can curl up and be surrounded by warmth.

If you are buying a bed that has sides, get one that is just big enough for your puppy to curl up in. Dogs often like to curl into little balls and burrow into bedding.

Look for bedding that says it is tough and resistant to chewing. Just remember that no bedding will be impossible to destroy. Inspect your puppy's bedding frequently to see if she is chewing it. If you get bedding that comes with filling of some type, a puppy could chew a hole in the outer covering and start pulling the stuffing out.

You may wish to have several beds scattered throughout the house. If you don't want your pets on the furniture, have a bed near the couch or chair where you spend a majority of your relaxing moments. This will provide a place that is comfortable for your pup and also allows her to be near the action of the family.

Food and Water Bowl

Your puppy will be happy eating out of anything that is nontoxic. Stainless steel and ceramic products are easy to clean and may resist chewing. Water bowls often become a source of fun, so find a bowl that the puppy cannot easily tip over.

Food-Dispensing Toys

Because puppies are such busy creatures, you may decide it is better to feed your puppy out of a food-dispensing toy. That way she spends time trying to get the food and has to engage her brain to problem solve how to make the food appear instead of just eating the food in less than five minutes and then looking for the next great adventure.

Collars

A collar and leash will be among your most important purchases, but the choices can be overwhelming. Spend some time checking out the variety of collars as well as harnesses, especially keeping in mind what your puppy will look like when she is grown up. A big dog like a Mastiff may be happier in a no-pull harness, while the Teacup Yorkie may be fine in just about anything.

A traditional collar, which just goes around the puppy's neck, is an awesome tool on which to attach identification tags. Even if your puppy is microchipped, having physical ID tags is important because it will help your puppy get back to you more quickly if she is found by a neighbor. If your puppy is a puller or you have a physical disability that makes any pressure on your arms uncomfortable, consider a no-pull harness rather than a collar.

The types of collars are endless, ranging from simple plastic to haute couture. If your puppy is less than 6 months old when you get her, you may wish to wait on the designer collar until she reaches her full growth. Most puppies go through one or two collars from the time they are 8 weeks old until they are 6 or 8 months old.

The buckle is one of the most important parts of a collar. You want a sturdy buckle that won't come apart if the puppy pulls hard on the collar. You also need something you can easily put on and take off. As you examine collars in the store, try the buckles and look at any stitching to ensure it is well made and will stand up to what you need.

Most traditional collars either have a buckle or a snap that holds the collar in place, as well as a way to adjust the size of the collar. A collar should be loose enough so you can slip your finger under it. As your puppy grows, you need to check your collar several times a week to ensure it isn't getting too tight. Take it off periodically so you can check the puppy's neck for irritation or chafing.

A martingale collar is a great option, especially for puppies whose necks are bigger than their heads. Many collars slip off if the puppy suddenly pulls backward. The martingale collar is designed to tighten slightly if a puppy pulls back on the leash; however, it can't overtighten and choke the puppy. When adjusted correctly, the martingale will tighten just enough to stop the puppy from pulling out of her collar, but when the pressure of the leash is released, the collar will expand slightly.

Choke chains, prong collars, and electric collars are never recommended for a puppy. A choke chain has no stop gap, so unlike a martingale collar, the choke chain will keep tightening on your puppy's neck. Prong collars have metal spikes that push into the dog's neck when it tightens. An electric collar delivers a shock to the puppy's neck. If you feel you cannot control your puppy without one of these devices, consult a professional trainer for more humane options.

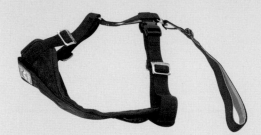

Harnesses

Many people choose harnesses for their dogs, and the variety can be astonishing. Harnesses can be an excellent option, because most of them take the pressure off the dog's neck. It is easy to damage a puppy's trachea or to cause his neck to become misaligned due to the pressure exerted by the puppy pulling on a leash. For tiny dogs, if their leashes are tight, their necks are often forced upward, again possibly causing future problems.

The larger the dog, the more thought you need to give to the type of harness you get. The wrong type of harness could turn a larger puppy into a pulling machine. Many harnesses have a D-ring on the top of the dog's back, to which you would attach the leash. For a strong puller, you basically just gave your dog the green light to become a sled dog and pull even harder, as these types of harnesses often provide a way for the dog to pull with her chest and front legs—both of which are very strong.

There are a number of excellent no-pull harnesses that take the pressure off the dog's neck and stop her from pulling, or at least lessen the pressure. A no-pull harness should be on only when the puppy is going for a walk. Harnesses can chafe, especially under the puppy's legs. Many harnesses are easy for the puppy to rip, so it is always better to just remove the harness when the puppy is not on a walk.

Seat Belt Harness

This harness is designed to keep your puppy restrained and safe in your car. The harness hooks to the seat belt itself or the seat belt mechanism.

No Pull Harness

These harnesses are designed to discourage the dog from pulling while walking. Use a harness only when your puppy is out for a walk, and watch for chafing.

Sport Harnesses

Some sports use a specific harness. The tracking harness, for example, is designed so the dog can lower her head to the ground so she can follow a track.

Leashes

Leashes come in almost as many varieties as collars. However, for most puppies a simple 4- or 6-foot (1.2 to 1.8m) leash will be just fine. You may want to invest in a 20- or 30-foot (6 to 12m) long line (a really long leash) for when you are teaching your puppy to come to you or if you want to play fetch with a very athletic dog.

Avoid using a retractable leash, which is sometimes referred to as a flexi leash. Many trainers agree that this type of leash just turns your puppy into a pulling machine because the puppy learns that every time she pulls, more leash comes out, which just teaches her to keep pulling. Another issue is that if you accidently drop the retractable leash, the handle is large and will bounce along the ground. This can frighten the puppy and cause her to run away because of the scary, bouncing handle that is "chasing" her. The handle could also actually hit the puppy and hurt her.

Toys

The variety of toys is endless, and the depth of your bank account is the only limit to what you can find to entertain your pup. But, before you go crazy in the toy aisle, take a deep breath and start with just a few choices. Just like children, some puppies are going to enjoy certain types of toys more than others. Also, having more toys doesn't mean your puppy will not be bored.

Puppies love to chew, so obviously toys they can chew on will engage their mouths and keep them off your ankles. Just be sure to supervise your puppy with a toy to make sure she isn't tearing off huge chunks of it. Puppies generally love things that squeak or toys that roll or bounce. A few squeaky toys, a ball, and toys designed for chewing are often your best bets to start with when the puppy first comes home.

There are also numerous toys designed to engage your puppy's mind, because a bored puppy is one that is going to be chewing up your couch. Puzzle toys are designed to teach the puppy to use her nose or her brain to figure out where a treat is hidden.

Once your puppy comes home and you can get a feel for the type of toys she enjoys, then you can go crazy shopping in the toy aisle. If you find your puppy tearing up your shoes, stealing your socks, etc., try to find toys that mimic what she finds so fascinating in the house. That way you can give her a toy that she enjoys instead of getting frustrated with her when she finds for herself toys she prefers.

Preparing Kids for a Puppy

If you have children, especially children under the age of 10, it is important that you spend time talking about what they should or should not do with the puppy. Many people have an idyllic view of kids and puppies happily cavorting together. But puppies most assuredly will nip or bite, and depending on their size, they can easily knock children down. Get a stuffed dog to help the children understand where to pet the puppy and what parts should be left alone. Show children how pulling the toy dog's ears and tail would hurt.

Avoiding Injuries

According to the ASPCA, there are 4.7 million dog bites per year in the United States, and more than half of those bites are to children. Bites from dogs are often to the face of a small child. While fatalities caused by dogs are extremely rare, and even bites requiring medical treatment are unusual, being bitten by the family pet can be devastating for both the parents and the child. It can be a life-ending event for the dog. Most bites are totally preventable with some management on the parent's part and vigilance in watching the puppy and child interact.

If you have children, become familiar with the signs of stress in a dog. If your children are old enough, talk to them about the signs of stress and teach them to give the puppy some space if they see those signs.

"Be a Tree"

Spend time teaching children to "be a tree." This is a program popularized by Doggone Safe (www. doggonesafe.com), a website dedicated to teaching children how to safely interact with dogs. The child's arms are her branches and her feet are the roots. To "be a tree," a child stops moving, folds her branches by crossing her arms, and looks down at her roots. It is good to practice being a tree before the puppy comes home. Dogs won't chase trees, but they will chase a running, squealing child. If a child learns to stop and be a tree whenever the dog is chasing her, most dogs calm down.

Avoiding Hazards and Escapes

Talk to the kids about the importance of keeping their toys and clothes picked up. If your children are too young to understand the dangers of accidentally allowing the puppy out whenever a door is opened, consider installing childproof door latches or add a baby gate across an entryway. If you put up a baby gate, teach the children to go through the gate without the puppy, and to not open the front door unless the puppy is safely behind the gate.

Preparing Other Pets for a Puppy

Before puppy comes home, there are things you can do to ensure smooth sailing when you introduce the puppy to his new animal family members.

Cats

If you have cats, make a cat safe room. For example, you could take a baby gate and put it across a door. Cats can jump over the baby gate, but the puppy can't get through. For larger puppies, you can put the baby gate a foot or so off the ground so the cats can go under the gate, but it still keeps the puppy out. Cats will learn that this room is a safe haven. It is also an excellent place to put your cat's litter box. Puppies absolutely love the litter box and digging out stinky cat poop. Using small pet doors that would allow your cat access to a room without allowing the puppy to follow will also work.

Make sure your cats also have a way to climb up and out of the reach of the puppy. Having one or two floor-to-ceiling cat trees spread throughout the house will ensure that the cat will have a safe haven to climb if it is being chased.

Older Dogs

If you have an older dog or a dog with physical limitations, consider how you can separate it from the puppy. While many dogs enjoy having a doggy friend, older dogs especially may not be so keen to have their sedentary life interrupted by a bundle of energy. For the first several months you will want to keep the puppy and other household pets separated when you can't be home to supervise. Have a plan in place for where the puppy and the resident dog will be when you aren't home.

Small Animals

Pet rabbits, rats, guinea pigs, and other small animals can be especially attractive to a puppy. It is often safest to keep pets like these in locations that can be made totally off-limits to the puppy. Even if a puppy co-exists with a rabbit when she is young, that doesn't mean that as she grows up she will continue to be friends with the rabbit.

Chapter 3

Bringing Puppy Home

- How to get your puppy home smoothly and safely and survive the first night
- Introducing the puppy to the family and pets
- Starting off the relationship right

It is an exciting day when you bring your puppy home. While you may have been planning this for months, it could be a day full of stress for the puppy. He will be traveling from a place he may have known well—and where he was comfortable—to a totally unknown environment. And chances are very good he has never ridden in a car before.

If your puppy is small and you have other people in the vehicle, holding him in your lap may be a good option. Take along some blankets or towels, because puppies pee or poop when nervous; and they can get carsick, especially on a first ride. Avoid passing the puppy around. Just rub his chin and neck to calm him down.

If you are alone or have a larger puppy, take a crate when picking him up so he can be safely contained. Trying to drive with a puppy walking around or climbing in your lap is dangerous. Avoid opening the windows to let him sniff the air. Puppies are fast, and you don't want him trying to jump out the window while you are driving.

When you get home, be sure the puppy is secured with a properly fitted collar and leash before you open the car door. Otherwise he might bolt from the car before anyone can stop him. Remember, the ride may have been very stressful for him and he might try to run away.

Clean house before the puppy comes home so you won't have to use the vacuum or dishwasher right away. Appliances can be scary, and you don't want your puppy hiding in terror.

Giving the Puppy Some Space

When you get the puppy home, the first thing you want to do is give him time to adjust. He needs time to get to know you and the rest of the family as well as to explore his new home. Avoid the urge to take him to visit every friend or relative you have. Ask the kids to wait a few days before they invite their friends over to meet the new family member. Don't make your first trip out with the puppy a trip to the veterinarian or the groomer. Wait a few days before you do anything potentially traumatic, such as giving the puppy his first bath.

Spending time letting your puppy adjust on his own schedule will help him get acclimated more quickly. If you overwhelm the puppy in his first few days with you, he could become anxious, which will make everything from housebreaking to socialization more difficult.

When you bring the puppy inside, let him explore at his own pace. He should not immediately meet other animals that live in the home. Basically, you want to leave him alone, but supervise him to ensure he doesn't get into trouble. Be sure to take him to his toilet area regularly.

If you find something in the house that scares the puppy, spend time assuring him that the scary object is really an opportunity to get awesome treats. Slick floors are often terrifying for puppies that have never walked on them before. If your puppy encounters a surface that he is reluctant to walk on, don't force him. Read Chapter 7 on socialization for tips on how to help the puppy overcome his fear of objects or flooring. Don't worry if it takes hours (or even days) for a puppy to decide to explore certain places. Going slow will mean the puppy will never come to view you or your home as scary.

Depending on the age of your puppy, you may also wish to avoid taking him anywhere lots of other dogs have been. Talk to your veterinarian about diseases such as parvo or parasite issues the puppy could be exposed to in public areas.

Be sure your puppy is wearing his collar with identification tags from the very moment he comes home. You don't want the puppy to become scared and bolt out the front door, but if he does, you want anyone who finds him to be able to return him to you.

Avoid the urge to pick up the puppy, kiss it, or hug it. It will be enough for the first week for the puppy to just get used to everyone, the house, the yard, and the other animal family members.

Meeting the Other Pets

If your household includes other pets, the key is to introduce them slowly. Let the puppy get used to the house and the yard before he gets to meet fellow canines or other animals. If you have dogs as well as other pets, start by introducing your puppy to your dogs first.

Meeting Other Dogs

There are many ways to introduce your puppy to the resident dog. The key component to all of them is that the dog and puppy need plenty of space to get away from each other. You want to make sure you aren't holding either dog or forcing them to be still. Dogs and puppies are very good at meeting as long as they are able to control the situation.

New pet owners are often embarrassed or alarmed if one dog starts humping or mounting another dog. Again, don't immediately step in and break this up. It is not a form of dominance—just a form of communication. It can be stress related or it can be an invitation to play.

Using a baby gate to separate them is one way for dogs to meet. Let the dogs sniff each other through the gate. Praise them both for good behavior. If one dog growls or seems anxious, avoid scolding the dog. You want him to communicate if he is uncomfortable. Give the dogs a few hours of seeing each other and sniffing. If they appear relaxed, they're ready to meet onleash. If one dog is lunging and growling and is not calming down, seek help from a professional trainer.

Another good way for dogs to meet is by going for a walk. Each dog should have his own person rather than one person trying to take both the puppy and the resident dog. You need for the dogs to be able to move closer or farther apart as needed. As you are walking, allow the dogs to sniff at each other briefly by keeping your leashes as loose as possible. If the dog or puppy appears anxious, move them farther apart. It is best if they can sniff front to tail rather than meeting face to face. Again, don't scold a dog for growling.

If the initial greeting on the walk or through the baby gate appears to be going well, it's time for the dogs to get acquainted. The best place for your puppy to meet the other dogs would be in a fenced yard. If that is not possible, have the dogs meet in the largest open space you have available. The space where your dogs meet for the first time should be free of food, treats, and toys of any kind.

Each dog should be wearing a long leash and have a well-fitted collar that won't slip off if you need to pull the dog away. If you have more than one dog, introduce the puppy to each dog individually before having them all meet as a group.

Each dog should have its own person holding a leash. The leashes should be as loose as possible and the dogs should be able to move toward or away from each other without feeling as if the human on the other end of the leash is dictating the direction the dog should go. Don't be alarmed if the dog and puppy don't instantly rush to each other and start playing. Dogs often want to circle, do lots of sniffing, and approach slowly.

As soon as you feel comfortable, drop the leashes. The dogs should still be dragging their leashes in case you need to intervene. Puppies can be extremely rude when meeting adult dogs. If your adult dog growls, lifts its lip, or air snaps at the puppy, don't rush in to stop that interaction. Adult dogs are generally extremely tolerant of puppies, but the puppy has to learn what is or is not appropriate. You want to see if the puppy backs off from the adult dog, even just momentarily. If it does, then the dogs are communicating.

If the puppy is pushy and will not leave the adult dog alone, be prepared to step in and interrupt the meeting. You don't want the adult dog to feel compelled to use his teeth to get the puppy to back off. It isn't fair to your older dog to force him to tolerate a puppy that refuses to be polite.

Once all the dogs have successfully met the puppy individually, then allow them all to meet in a group. Just keep the leashes on so you can control the situation if necessary. If you are worried about an interaction, separate the dogs and see what the puppy does. If it hides, go back a few steps in your introduction. If it comes back out and wants to interact, things were most likely going well. If the situation becomes overly stressful, use the leashes to move the dogs rather than grab the dogs' collars.

Keep initial meetings short. Even if the dogs are playing and appear to be having a great time, there is a very thin line between play that is fun and play that starts to get rough. Never leave your puppy and the resident dogs alone together for any length of time until you are absolutely sure they get along. It is far better to leave the dogs crated or separated in some other way, at least until the puppy is fully grown and you have a better idea of the group dynamics of the various household dogs.

Once the dogs and puppy seem to be interacting well, gradually introduce resources. Start by offering the older dog and the puppy each a treat while they are side by side. Introduce a toy while the dogs are still dragging leashes so you can pull them apart if one dog doesn't want to share the toy with the others. Don't feed the puppy and the resident dogs near each other. Give everyone plenty of space. Don't let the puppy attempt to eat from the older dog's dish.

Many dogs are naturally resource guarders, and you never know what might be a resource. Some dogs may be fine sharing a toy, but not a dropped tissue. Humans often become a valued resource, and some dogs may try to warn other dogs away from a person by growling or attacking a dog that comes near the coveted human.

Consult a dog-training professional immediately if your puppy and older dog have any issues with sharing.

Meeting the Cat

When your puppy meets your cat for the first time, the pup should drag a leash. Don't let the puppy rush the cat and cause the cat to run. You want the cat to feel comfortable being around the puppy, and running cats are often too hard for a puppy to resist chasing.

Use a can of tuna to keep your cat in the room with the puppy. Allow the puppy to see the cat, and reward the puppy with treats if he is polite. Also reward the cat for being near the puppy. If the cat hisses or swats at the puppy, don't interfere immediately. You want to see if the puppy learns to respect the cat asking him to back off. Reward the puppy for when he sees the cat and ignores it.

Don't allow the puppy to chase the cat. While it might be cute when the puppy is small, if you don't want him to chase the cat when he is an adult, don't allow the practice to start. However, there are some cats and dogs that love to play together. It will be up to you to determine whether the puppy and cat are having fun together or if the cat is becoming stressed. If the cat continually leaves the room when the puppy enters, the cat is not having a good time.

Teach the puppy that when the cat is in the room and he doesn't chase it, great treats happen. If the cat leaves the room, the treats go away. Many puppies will learn that leaving a cat alone is more rewarding than chasing it.

Unfortunately, animals that run often invoke a prey response from the dog. Some dogs seem more predisposed to chase a running cat than others. Sighthounds such as Greyhounds and Whippets are bred to hunt game by sight rather than scent. Many hunting dogs also seem to have issues with cats and other household pets. But there are also plenty of success stories with these types of dogs living harmoniously with cats. Each puppy is an individual, but if you start from the very beginning teaching the puppy that leaving the cat alone is more rewarding than chasing it, your chances of cat and dog living in peace will be greatly improved.

Until you are absolutely convinced that your puppy will not harm your cat, never leave the puppy alone with it. Remember to always have a safe room for the cat where it can go to escape the puppy.

Meeting Small Pets

While the internet is full of cute photos of puppies snuggling next to rabbits, guinea pigs, and other small pets, the reality is that dogs don't necessarily understand these creatures are part of the family. The younger the puppy, the better your chances of getting him to understand that the rabbit is more valuable if it is left alone. Give the puppy high-value training treats for ignoring a pocket pet.

But never become complacent and imagine that your puppy loves your bunny in the same way you do. Nothing can be more devastating to a family than to find that one pet has severely injured or killed another. The bottom line is you have a dog, and dogs are hunters. It is generally safer if puppies and small mammals or birds are kept separated. Never underestimate the lengths a dog will go to in order to get to a caged pet.

Meeting Family Members

A puppy circle is a great way for the puppy to meet the family. Have family members sit in a circle outdoors or in a room with lots of space. Make sure everyone has dog treats and wait for the puppy to come up to the people in the circle. Avoid calling the puppy or making a lot of noise. Remember, dogs read body language cues instead of understanding what you are saying. When the puppy goes to a person, she should open her hand and give the puppy a treat. The next person in the circle should then show the puppy that he or she has a treat, and soon the puppy will learn that going up to each person will result in something fun.

If the puppy is wiggly and engaged, have family members begin to pet her when she comes by for the treat. If the puppy seems nervous or is backing away from people, spread the circle out and just give the pup a bit more time.

Introducing the Puppy to the Kids

There is absolutely no doubt that most children love puppies. If your home includes children, especially under the age of 10, you'll need to spend a lot of time helping them and the puppy learn some basic rules. Don't allow the child and puppy to get into bad habits when the puppy is small. As she grows, she won't understand why the game that was fun when she was 10 pounds is no longer tolerated when she weighs 50 pounds.

You should never leave a young child alone with a dog. The younger the child, the more supervision you must provide. All dogs will bite given the right circumstances. For children old enough to follow rules, establish guidelines about what is appropriate and inappropriate. Older children might be responsible enough to play more games with the puppy and take an active role in her training.

Consistency Is Key

When meeting other family members, consistency is the key. All the family must learn to train the puppy in the same way. If one family member allows the puppy to jump up and gives her lots of love when she jumps up, but another yells or pushes her when she jumps up, the puppy will be very confused about what is wanted.

Likewise, if one person in the family allows the puppy to pull constantly on a leash during walks, but another wants the puppy to walk beside her, again, the puppy will have no idea what is correct. Have a family meeting to discuss training the puppy to avoid unwanted behaviors caused by each person doing his or her own thing.

If your family includes a person with a disability, teach the puppy to be calm around that person by rewarding good behavior. Wheelchairs and walkers can be scary to a puppy. Go slow and reward the puppy for being calm in the presence of such devices from a distance and gradually work up to having the puppy get closer to the objects.

Getting Through the First Night

The first night at home with the puppy may very well set the tone for the rest of your life together. Hopefully, you got the puppy at a time when you can spend time teaching it to love its crate. Even if you later want the pup to sleep with you, having it spend its first nights in the crate may be beneficial for housebreaking purposes. This first night may be hard for both of you. If possible, get the puppy during a time when you won't be inconvenienced by a few nights of less-than-normal sleep.

Put the puppy's crate in an area where it will be convenient for you to take her out for a potty break in the night and in a location where you can easily hear her.

When you put the puppy to bed for the night, give her something to chew on that will take her mind off the fact that you are leaving her. Ignore those heart-wrenching whimpers and cries the puppy is sure to make. If you talk to her, go back to comfort her, or even yell at her to be quiet, the puppy will have learned she can control her interactions with you. The puppy needs to learn that the only way you will come back is if she is quiet.

If your puppy is under 5 months of age, set your alarm so you get up halfway through the night to let her out for a potty break. If she is less than 3 months of age, be prepared to get up more than once. You want to take her out before she cries and wakes you up. Some puppies quickly learn that whining or barking makes you get up and take them out. This won't be fun later if she just wants to go out for a romp in the yard. This is a delicate balancing act, as you don't want to ignore a puppy that is crying because she needs out to potty. However, you also don't want to teach a puppy that crying makes you get out of bed for a walk in the yard.

If you find that your puppy is whining and you take her out and she doesn't potty, put her back in the crate, wait 20 minutes or so, and take her back out and see if she will go. If she continually whines but won't potty, just ignore her the next time and take her out on a schedule you set.

If the puppy is frantic or is injuring herself trying to get out of the crate, consult your veterinarian or a professional dog trainer.

As the puppy gets older, you will need to take her out less and less during the night.

Avoid playing with the puppy on nighttime outings. Be calm and quiet, put her on a leash, reward her for going potty, and take her right back into the crate. You want the puppy to learn that going outside will not be full of fun and games. It is strictly for business.

Bonding with Your Puppy

The more you do with your puppy, the more she will come to view you as fun. All family members should interact with her to the extent their age allows. Often a family will contact a trainer complaining that the puppy only listens to a certain family member. This is generally the person who feeds her, walks her, or spends the most time with her.

The first three months with your puppy can be crucial in terms of setting the tone for your life together. Make sure the puppy has only positive experiences with you. Even though she is going to exasperate you, avoid yelling at her or doing anything that she could perceive as scary.

Be sure that every time your puppy comes to you, she gets a reward. Even if you don't have treats, use your voice or lots of scratches to her chin to let her know that checking in with you is an awesome idea.

While it is great to set aside time each day for specific training, be prepared to reward your dog anytime you catch her doing something you like. Here is a fun game for bonding:

Sit on the floor with a handful of small treats and show the puppy a treat.

Throw the treat a few feet away.

Show her another treat and have her run back to you for the reward. She will soon learn to run out and get the thrown treat and then run right back to you for the next one.

Hide the treat sometimes so she doesn't see it in your hand, and surprise her with it when she runs back. You want her to begin to learn that coming back to you is a good idea whether she sees a treat or not. Throw a toy sometimes when she comes back or reward her with praise or a scratch under the chin.

Learning to Be Happy While Not Playing

Teach your puppy that it is fun to lie on a bed beside the couch while you watch TV or read a book. Give her a long-lasting chew on her bed when you first sit down. This will help her understand that just because you aren't interacting with her, it doesn't mean life isn't awesome.

Play Should Begin and End with You

Avoid future issues by always initiating play rather than letting your puppy bring you a toy for play. It is super cute when she waddles up to you with a toy in her mouth. But when she is older she may not understand that you don't have time to play right that second. Teach her that you will play with her a lot, but play begins and ends with you. This is especially important if you have a puppy obsessed with playing fetch. Fetch is fun when you have time for it, but if you are fixing dinner and the puppy constantly drops a toy at your feet, it can get annoying.

Setting Rules for Kids and Puppies

The top two rules for kids: never follow a puppy that walks away, and never corner a puppy. If a puppy walks away from a child, she may be stressed and trying to get away. Trapping a puppy in a situation where she has no escape route could cause her to feel threatened enough to bite.

Puppies should not be picked up and carried, and contrary to popular belief, most puppies do not enjoy being hugged. Children should be taught not to pull a puppy's tail or ears, and rules should be made to allow the puppy to eat in an area free from kids too young to understand not to bother her while she is eating.

Rules for Play

Young children should never play tug games or any game that involves placing a hand near the puppy's muzzle. Running and chasing games are fun for the puppy, and most children have fun until the puppy knocks them down or bites them. For this reason, children should be taught not to play run-and-chase games. See Chapter 12 for good ideas for appropriate play.

Teach a child that if a puppy is chasing her, she should stand still, fold her arms across her chest, and look at her feet. By folding her arms, she is taking her hands out of the way of puppy's teeth. By looking at her feet, she is ignoring the puppy—in effect, telling it to go away. If a puppy gets overexcited and will not stop nipping at a child's legs or arms, the parent should teach the child to go into a room and close the door until the parent can calm the situation.

Under no circumstance should children be allowed to hit or kick a puppy. If the puppy is sleeping, children should leave her alone or call to her from a few feet away so she can wake up and come to them. Do not allow puppies to lick children in the face. Children should not try to ride or play dress-up games with the puppy.

For the first few weeks after the puppy comes home, you and your children should spend time training her each day. When you can't supervise, the puppy should be in her crate or separated from the kids by a baby gate.

Keep the Kid Toys Safe

Most toys look the same to a puppy, and he may decide the children's toys look fun. One client told her trainer about a situation in which a 4-year-old was swinging a doll around by its arm. A young Boxer saw the doll and thought it was a fun tug toy. The dog grabbed the doll's arm and pulled, which caused the 4-year-old to scream and pull back. From the dog's perspective, they were playing a fun game; from the child's perspective, her beloved doll was being torn up. She dropped the doll and kicked at the dog. Luckily, the dog ran away and adults intervened immediately.

Don't Tempt the Puppy with Food

Another issue often arises when kids are eating or walking with food in their hands, and the puppy jumps at them to get the food. If a child is walking with food, the puppy might jump to get it and nip the child's fingers. Mealtimes may be a good time for the puppy to be in her crate, and children should be taught to never tease a puppy with food.

Don't allow young children to feed a puppy treats. They should be old enough to understand how to offer the treat on a flat palm rather than with their fingers. Young children often reach out with a treat, get scared when the puppy jumps for it, and pull their arm back, teaching the puppy to jump quicker and higher to get the treat. Holding the treat on a flat palm teaches the puppy to lick it off the hand rather than grab it.

The bottom line is, always supervise youngsters and puppies, and teach the children to be kind. This also goes for your children's friends. Always make sure any child who is visiting knows how to behave around the puppy.

Chapter 4

Feeding Your Puppy

- Dry, canned, raw, and natural foods
- Feeding amounts and schedules
- Keeping your puppy hydrated
- Which foods are ideal puppy treats

An important part of adding a puppy to your family is to make sure you have the right nutrition available to help him grow to his maximum potential. Proper nutrition is essential for healthy bones and muscles, a good coat, bright eyes, and plenty of puppy energy. Along with a nutritious diet, you will also need to establish a regular schedule for feeding your puppy.

There are many ways to meet all of your puppy's nutritional needs. Take your time to research a good diet choice for your puppy before he comes home. Ask his breeder for suggestions. Most good breeders will send home some of the same food your puppy has been eating so there is no abrupt change. If the pup is coming from a shelter, ask what food they have been feeding him.

If you change the puppy's diet from what the breeder or shelter was feeding him, you will need to do so gradually. Feed the original food for at least the first three days, and then start adding in the new food at a ratio of 25 percent to 75 percent. After three days on that ratio, switch to a 50:50 ratio. Give the puppy another three days and move on to 75 percent new food with 25 percent original food. In three more days your puppy will be totally on the new food.

Your veterinarian can provide advice on a proper diet for your new family member. Animal and veterinary nutritionists, who specialize in balancing diets for pets, can also help you find the perfect foods for your puppy. A good diet will include the right amount and right balance of proteins, fats, carbohydrates, vitamins, and minerals, as well as plenty of fresh water. Skimping on any of these or feeding an unbalanced ratio can lead to permanent health problems.

Dry Foods

Dry foods may seem boring, but they have many advantages for feeding a puppy if you do your homework and find the right food. Dry food might not look as appealing as canned or home-cooked foods, but your puppy is more interested in taste than appearance.

The Pluses

There are many pluses to feeding dry foods like kibbles, and convenience is a big one. Kibble can be easily packed for trips, and most brands are easy to find if you purchase food as you travel. Kibble does not require refrigeration or any fancy preparation. Dry food can also help with your dog's dental care.

There are many different brands, flavors, and types of dry foods, so it is likely you can find one that your puppy likes to eat and that also fulfills his nutritional requirements. Dry foods may be less expensive than canned foods, though top-quality foods are always a bit pricier.

The Minuses

Most dry foods contain some grains. While many dogs do fine (and in fact some do best) on foods containing grains, others do not. Certain breeds, such as Irish Setters, may suffer gluten intolerance and don't do well on foods with wheat. Other puppies may be sensitive to corn. There are dry foods without grains, but they may take some searching. Most foods can be ordered online if your local pet supply store doesn't carry what your puppy needs.

Ingredients

It is important that you check the label to be sure the food contains all the proper nutrients. The label will include the ingredients listed in order by weight. A list that starts with a meat protein is generally best. If the list includes two or three versions of a grain—such as whole corn, corn meal, and so on—they may add up to much more than the chicken listed as the first ingredient. Always choose a food labeled for puppies or that says it is nutritionally complete for all life stages.

INGREDIENTS

Beef, beef meal, lamb meal, potatoes, egg, sunflower oil, buffalo, lamb, venison, beef cartilage, herring oil, apples, carrots, garlic, tomatoes, vitamins, natural flavors, dried chicory root, lecithin, rosemary extract

GUARANTEED ANALYSIS

Crude Protein (minimum)	42.0%
Crude Fat (minimum)	22.0%
Crude Fiber (maximum)	2.5%
Linoleic Acid (minimum)	1.2%
Vitamin E (minimum)	250 IU/kg
Omega-3 Fatty acids* (minimum)	0.40%
Total Microorganisms* (minimum)	40,500,000 CFU/kg

* Not recognized as an essential nutrient by the AAFCO Dog Food Nutrient Profiles

Feeding Guidelines for Your Puppy by Size

Large-breed puppies have benefited from research into the exact balance of nutrients needed for their rapid growth. Special attention has to be paid to the protein level as well as the exact calcium and phosphorus balance for a large-breed puppy like a Great Dane or an Irish Wolfhound. For this reason, you might choose a food designed just for large-breed puppies. A diet that is labeled for all puppies or complete and balanced for all life stages may be adequate, but you will need to be careful about the amounts you feed for your puppy's weight.

Small-size puppies may need extra feedings throughout the day to maintain proper blood sugar levels. It is better to use their regular diet for these extra meals—not treats that may not contain proper nutrients.

The American Academy of Veterinary Nutrition provides extensive links to resources for pet owners at their website: http://aavn.org/.

Finicky Eaters

Some puppies will be finicky eaters and turn up their nose at dry chow. In addition, puppies going through teething may have sensitive gums and be hesitant to chew anything hard. You can easily mix some warm water in with your puppy's food to increase the odor and soften the food a bit. Some puppies really enjoy the gravy this creates. Always make sure that the food is not hot when you give it to your puppy.

You can also add a teaspoon or two of canned food. Be sure the canned food is also nutritionally complete or made for puppies. Throw away any dry food that has been moistened or has had canned food added if your puppy doesn't eat it all at once.

Canned Foods

Canned foods tend to appeal to many owners. Enticing labels such as "Mom's Own Pot Roast Dinner" or "Turkey Deluxe" can get human salivary glands flowing, let alone a puppy's.

The Pluses

Most puppies will dig right into a dish of canned food. The smells and texture are very attractive. Canned food will provide some extra moisture if you have a pup who doesn't drink much. And canning is a very safe way to preserve most foods. Canned foods can be excellent for enticing a finicky puppy to eat. There are many canned foods to choose from, and most are easy to find. You should be able to find a flavor your puppy likes and a brand that fits his nutritional requirements.

The Minuses

Canned foods can be quite expensive. This is especially true if you have a larger-size puppy. Puppies can rapidly gulp down a bowl of canned food, and they may still act hungry right after eating. Canned foods should also be balanced and complete with all the vital nutrients for all life stages, or labeled specifically for puppies. Canned foods need to be refrigerated after opening. Refrigerated food can be less palatable and may need to be warmed a bit. Canned food requires more packaging than dry food, but it can be recycled.

Know Your Labels!

Dog foods can be a bit deceptive in their labeling.

- Food labeled as **"beef"** must contain 95 percent beef, not counting water added f
- Food labeled as **"beef dinner"** may contain anywhere from 25 to 95 percent beef
- Food labeled as **"dog food with beef"** may contain as little as 3 percent beef.
- Food labeled as **"beef flavor"** needs to contain only enough beef to be detectable.

These guidelines apply to all pet foods—dry and canned.

Protein Sources

Dogs are certainly carnivores, but they're also somewhat omnivorous when it comes to food. The ideal protein source for their diet is animal protein. That means meat of various types along with eggs, and some dairy products for dogs who tolerate dairy. Various combinations of grains can come very close to providing complete proteins for dogs as well, but meat is the best. Popular sources of meat are chicken, beef, lamb, and fish. Less common sources include venison, rabbit, duck, and bison.

Food Allergies

True food allergies are not common in dogs. Real allergies tend to show up as ear infections and skin conditions. More common are food intolerances, leading to stomach upsets, gas, and diarrhea. If your puppy consistently has loose stool but no parasites, consider switching to a food with a different protein source. That may be all he needs!

Food Safety

Canned foods tend to be quite safe due to processing; however, you do need to take some care when choosing your puppy's food. Avoid cans with dents or with bulges at the top or bottom. Check expiration dates. These may be on the paper labels or on the bottom of the can itself.

Pet Food Recalls

Considering how much pet food is manufactured on a daily basis, recalls are not that common. Many recalls are done on a voluntary basis before any pets become ill. If your puppy's food is included in a recall, stop feeding it immediately, even if he has been acting fine. Then contact the company or your retailer.

Raw or Home-Cooked Foods

Cooking for your puppy or feeding him raw foods are two increasingly popular options for providing the proper nutrition. Both of these options can work, but require some extra research and diligence on your part.

A Balanced Diet

Feeding your puppy home-cooked food properly takes more than a handy saucepan and some bacon. Due to their rapid growth rate, puppies need just the right amounts and balance of nutrients. Even home-cooked or raw diets that have been balanced by a veterinary nutritionist may not be adequate or appropriate for your puppy.

Do Your Homework

There are veterinary nutritionists at most veterinary colleges and there are websites such as BalanceIT.com that can provide support and recipes. Your puppy will not do well if he is only fed meat (raw or cooked). He needs other vitamins and minerals for healthy development.

Supplementing

Most home-cooked and raw diets will require some supplements to completely balance your puppy's nutrition. These supplements should be specifically designed for puppies. There are some that are made for large-breed versus small-breed puppies. Do not use additional supplements without consulting your veterinarian or a veterinary nutritionist.

Proper Hygiene

Whether cooking for your family or your puppy, you need to practice good food safety and hygiene. Clean up thoroughly with hot water, soap, and bleach after preparing raw meat. Thaw meats in the refrigerator. If cooking meat, heat it to the recommended temperature, gauging this with a meat thermometer.

Pluses of a Home-Cooked Diet

- There are meals you can make for both your human family and your puppy to eat.
- Puppies enjoy home-cooked meals—even the finicky eaters!
- Human-grade ingredients supply top-quality nutrition.
- With a home-cooked meal plan, you know exactly what your puppy is eating.

Minuses of a Home-Cooked Diet

- To ensure adequate nutrition, you need outside help in the form of recipes.
- You may need to purchase supplements to make sure your puppy has optimum fuel for growth.
- Planning and cooking meals takes time.
- You need to plan ahead for any trips.

Pluses of a Raw Diet

- You are coming as close as possible to a "natural" diet.
- Most dogs enjoy a raw diet.
- Dogs who are sensitive to preservatives do well on a raw diet.
- If nothing else, most puppies enjoy getting to chew on a raw, meaty bone!
- You will know exactly what your puppy is eating.

Minuses of a Raw Diet

- Puppies cannot grow properly and be healthy on strictly raw meat; they need supplements and other nutrients.
- Feeding raw foods can increase the risk of illness to infants and people with immunocompromised health.
- Locating sources for ingredients and storing and preparing them safely take extra time and effort.

Combining Puppy Food Options

Feeding your puppy does not have to be an either-or situation. Many puppy owners successfully do a combination of dry and canned food, or dry and home-cooked, and so on. If you do decide to mix and match, be sure that both components are appropriate and adequate for a puppy. Do not do an abrupt switch from a raw diet to dry kibble for a trip. That could be a recipe for disaster!

Recipes for home-cooked or raw diets may be found online at the nutrition department of many veterinary colleges. Some pet food companies will provide free recipes for home-made meals and treats. The National Academy of Sciences offers some extensive pet nutrition information for dogs of all ages.

Natural Foods

Feeding natural foods is a common desire for families with puppies. Natural is generally considered healthier. But the question then becomes, just what does "natural" mean?

According to the FDA

The FDA (Food and Drug Administration) basically feels no foods are truly natural because they have all been processed to some degree. If a food does not have added color, artificial flavors, or any synthetic substances such as artificial preservatives, the FDA will allow it to officially be labeled as "natural."

According to Your Puppy

Puppies have a much broader definition of what is natural. For a puppy, chewing on sticks, eating animal poop, and scarfing up the remnants of a dead animal found on a walk all come under the heading of natural. It is your responsibility to oversee what entices your puppy and keep him away from dangerous or unhealthy choices.

Checking Labels

You can still try to keep your pup's diet as natural as possible without adding sticks. One easy way is to look for natural preservatives on the ingredient list. Any foods with fats will require antioxidants to keep them from going rancid. A natural source would be mixed tocopherols or a form of vitamin E. If the ingredients are foreign to you or use too many letter acronyms without spelling the exact ingredient, they are probably not natural.

Organic Choices

Organic designations are also headaches for regulatory groups like the FDA. There are no black-and-white rules for the meaning of "organic" in pet foods at this time. Organic suggests that the plants and animals used to manufacture a food were raised under certain conditions—ideally without herbicides, pesticides, and artificial hormones. Organic food choices tend to be more expensive, as it is generally more labor intensive to raise the plants and animals.

Free-Range and Grass-Fed

Free-range and grass-fed refer to methods of animal husbandry for meat-producing animals as well as eggs from ducks and chickens. With a true free-range setup, poultry run loose during the day, eating bugs and scavenging plants and weeds as well as being fed their prepared grains. Grass-fed beef and lamb means the animals are raised on pasture and not usually given any grain. In some cases, grain will be added toward the end of their growth time. Grass-fed meat tends to be leaner and somewhat more nutritious than grain-fed meat.

Avoid foods whose ingredients include preservatives such as ethoxyquin, BHA (butylated hydroxyanisole), or BHT (butylated hydroxytoluene). It is best to choose foods with natural preservatives, such as alpha tocopherols or ascorbate, which are forms of vitamins E and C.

How Much to Feed Your Puppy

How much to feed your puppy will be an ever-changing amount for the first two to twelve months. It is a very individual decision, affected by the type of food, the pup's activity level, and his growth rate. With help from your veterinarian, and your breeder if your puppy is a purebred, you can work out how much food he needs for optimum growth.

How Round Should He Be?

A round, bouncing puppy always looks so cute. In reality, you do not want a chubby pup. Added weight during the developmental stages can be harmful to the growing bones and joints. You should be able to feel your puppy's ribs and see a "waist" when you look down at him.

Size Matters

A giant-breed puppy will clearly need more food than a toy breed. When worked out on a per-pound basis, however, that is generally not true. Small puppies may burn more energy to keep warm, and often have higher metabolism rates. They also need top-quality nutrition because they can't eat a large amount at one time.

Quality Matters

If you are feeding a top-notch, premium diet, you will feed a smaller amount than if you feed lesser-quality food. In the end the cost will generally even out. A top-quality food will not require any supplements to help your puppy grow. Your pet needs and deserves the best!

Mixing and Matching Foods

Determining the exact amount that's right for your puppy can be tricky if you mix types of foods. If you decide to combine canned and dry foods, for example, start off by using half the recommended amounts on each label. You will need to weigh your puppy weekly—a good idea anyway—and check his body condition to see if you need to adjust amounts.

Guidance Only

The reality is that feeding instructions on labels are only guidelines. You will need to adjust your puppy's intake up or down based on his activity level and individual body condition score. If your puppy has been out playing in the snow with you, he may need extra calories at his next meal. If he spent the day snoring by the couch, he may be better off with slightly less food.

Read Labels

Pet foods have feeding instructions on the labels, and most give instructions based on weight. Because your puppy is constantly growing, the amount will have to be adjusted as his weight increases. Veterinary clinics will allow your puppy to visit weekly for "weigh ins" on their scales if this is not convenient at home.

Breed Is a Factor

Your puppy's breed can also figure into how fast he burns up calories. Most Labrador Retrievers are an example of an "easy keeper" breed. Those puppies tend to do well on almost any food. Many of the sighthound breeds are much harder to convince to eat and to keep a decent weight on. The combination of breeds in your mixed breed will influence his growth rate as well.

Frequent Feedings

Very young puppies, say less than 3 months of age, do best with four small meals a day. That can go down to three meals a day from 3 to 6 months. Most puppies do well with two meals a day after 6 months. Some very small breeds may still need extra snacks to keep their blood sugar levels up.

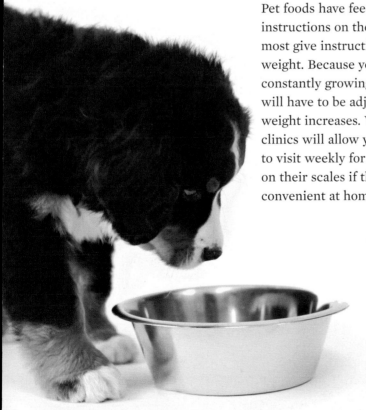

Appetite as a Guide

Your puppy's appetite can be a rough guide to the feeding amount. If your puppy polishes off his meal in less than a minute and is licking the bowl or looking around for more, you may need to increase the amount a bit. If he walks away satisfied and leaves some food in his bowl, you should cut back a little.

Setting a Feeding Schedule

Determining a feeding schedule for your puppy will be an ever-changing task as your puppy matures. Young puppies need more frequent feedings, while older ones can do well on fewer. Your work schedule will have to factor in as well. The goal is to be as consistent as you can and make sure your puppy's nutritional needs are met for optimal growth and development.

Two to Three Months

Most puppies of this age do best with four daily meals. Think early morning, noon, late afternoon, and late evening. Toy breed and very small puppies may need an additional snack or two to keep their blood sugar up. Some pups do best with a fourth meal through 4 months of age.

Three to Six Months

Puppies of this age tend to thrive on three meals a day. Figure breakfast, lunch, and dinner, just like your schedule. This may still mean going home at lunchtime if you work away from home, or arranging for a friend or neighbor to help you out.

Six to Twelve Months

From 6 to 12 months of age, most puppies do well on two meals a day. Small breeds may still need a third meal or at least a midday snack. Most adult dogs do best on two meals a day, so plan to continue this schedule for the rest of your dog's life if possible.

What Goes In, Comes Out

Your puppy's feeding and housetraining schedules are going to overlap. Usually a puppy will eliminate within 20 to 30 minutes after eating. Be sure to allow time in the schedule for your puppy to be walked after he eats. Water should be available at each feeding as well.

Use Your Feeding Time Wisely

Feeding time can be an excellent time to work in a little training for your puppy. Use part of his food to do some training work before he eats the main meal. He will be hungry and eager to "work for food." Short training sessions are best for puppies, so a quick sit or down before meals is perfect.

No Days Off

Remember that your puppy has no concept of weekends or vacation days. He will expect to hold to the same feeding schedule seven days a week. Once he is over 6 months old you may get some breaks, but many dogs hold to a schedule even as adults. A routine schedule is also important while housetraining.

Adjustments

If you know your work schedule is going to change, try to gradually shift your puppy's schedule as well. Doing gradual shifts will be better for his housetraining, too. There will be days when things don't flow smoothly. Just accept that your pup may not eat all his food on those days, or may have accidents. Having a set place for meals is good for your puppy, too. He can eat in peace and will learn the routine of eating there. A crate is an ideal place to feed him.

Diet Adjustments

Be aware that changes in your puppy's diet may also mean some turbulence in your schedule. Even switching flavors within a brand can cause mild stomach upset or diarrhea. If you need to switch, try to do so gradually. If possible, keep the timing on your schedule the same, so the change in diet is the only difference. Puppies do best with minimal adjustments.

Travel Plans

If your puppy will be accompanying you on a trip, make an effort to keep his feeding schedule steady. He won't understand about time zone changes. Fussiness, not eating well, and housetraining problems can all crop up during travel. Be patient and understanding.

Finding Help

Some dog sitters will do visits to help with puppy feedings and housetraining. The cost is worth it for the peace of mind for you and the comfort of your pup. Look for bonded, certified dog sitters and interview them. Make sure your puppy is comfortable with the person who will be helping.

How Much Water Does a Puppy Need?

Water provides essential nutrients for your puppy. He must drink adequate water or he will get dehydrated and could even die. Fresh, clean water should always be readily available.

Water Bowls

Provide stainless steel or ceramic bowls for your puppy's water. Unlike rubber and plastic bowls, these are unlikely to cause allergic reactions. They are also easy to clean and transport. Base the size of your pup's water bowl on his size. Too big and he could drown if he falls in. Too small and he won't get enough to drink.

Minimizing Spills

When choosing water bowls, look for sturdy ones with a heavy base. You also can find holders that attach to a feeder base or to a crate to keep a bowl upright. Gravity water bottles like those used for rabbits can also work for puppies.

Fresh Water

At a minimum, plan on putting fresh water in the bowl every time you feed your puppy. Rinse the bowl with each fill and wash it daily. Don't simply top it off with added water—use totally fresh water. The same rules apply to the drinking bottles that hang on the cage.

Availability

Ideally your puppy would have a fresh bowl of water available at all times. That would also mean someone available to take him outside to eliminate at all times, too. In real life, that often is not the case. Make sure your puppy has water before and after every meal. Plan his evening drinking around your housetraining schedule.

Water Playtime Solutions

Some puppies love to play in their drinking water. They put their paws in, jump in the bowl, flip it, or even pick it up and run with it. Sturdy or attached bowls can help to minimize this playing. You can also consider either putting ice cubes in the bowl or freezing a bowl of water to put in the crate or exercise pen. That way you minimize spills and provide fresh, cool water as the ice slowly melts.

Reluctant Drinkers

If you find your puppy is not drinking much, there are ways to increase consumption. You can add some water to his meals. Do this gradually; some puppies like soggy food and others will turn their noses up. If you soften food, throw out any leftovers.

There are flavor solutions you can add to water to encourage drinking. Check with your veterinarian to be sure they are suitable for a puppy. A couple of drops of water from a can of tuna can also add flavor. Some pups will also drink more water if you put an ice cube in the bowl.

Weather and Water

It's obvious that a puppy will need plenty of water during warm weather. If he plays outside or goes for a walk in hot weather, be sure he has fresh, cool water to drink. Take water and a portable drinking bowl on long walks. Remember, if he drinks a lot while playing outside, your puppy will also need to urinate more.

Puppies need plenty of fresh water in winter, too. If they eat snow for fluids, they will lose body heat. Many heating systems provide little humidity. Your pup will need to drink more due to the dry air.

Treats

Every puppy will get treats at some time. People love to feed their puppies, and treats are also used for training and to quiet a puppy at nap time or bedtime. Proper use of treats can enhance the human-animal bond. Some commonsense rules need to be applied when it comes to puppies and treats, though.

How Many?

How many treats are too many? Figure that your puppy's treats should never equal more than 10 percent of his diet. Beyond that amount, you risk unbalancing his diet and causing digestive upsets. Dogs can count (at least up to 6 or so), so if your puppy is used to getting two biscuits at bedtime and you need to cut back, simply break one biscuit in half. Your puppy doesn't have a sense of volume, so he will feel he is getting his fair share with the two pieces.

Using Food as Treats

An easy way to maintain a nutritious diet but still use some treats is to simply keep some of his regular food reserved for treats and training. You will get the maximum benefit from the puppy's diet and he will enjoy some extra attention and training.

Table Food?

Some veterinarians are firmly convinced that your puppy should never get any table scraps or "people food" treats. The reality is that he will get some human food sooner or later. Try to restrict treats to healthy food. Give him some small pieces of cut-up chicken or steak without fat. Some puppies enjoy chewing on a piece of raw carrot, especially when they are teething. Remember the rule about not going over 10 percent of the diet with treats.

Do not give any treats while you are sitting at the dinner table. This will teach your pup to beg. Wait until your meal is over, then move away from the table and either use the treat for a quick training exercise or put it in his food bowl. You want to instill good habits right from the beginning.

Homemade Treats

Baking your own dog treats can be a fun activity for your family. There are many recipes that provide healthy and fun treats for your puppy. Most of these are not nutritionally balanced, so they aren't a substitute for a regular diet. You can find cute cookie cutters in various dog themes. Your pup might like to hand out bone-shaped treats at his puppy class graduation. You can also make your own chicken jerky by simply slicing chicken breasts thinly and baking them to crispness in your oven. A dehydrator can also be used to make safe meat treats.

Treats to Avoid

Avoid treats that have been dyed, such as treats with red dyes. Soft, moist foods and treats are not always healthy for your puppy. Always check the ingredients just as you do for your puppy's regular diet. It's best to choose only treats that you know are made in your own country.

Holidays and Visitors

Always monitor visitors and holiday guests in your home to limit the amount and types of treats guests, especially small children, feed your puppy. Otherwise you will be dealing with stomach and intestinal upsets. Your puppy will be perfectly happy if you break a small treat into two or three pieces so visitors can share with him. And don't leave food or snacks where a puppy can reach them. Some snacks for people, such as macadamia nuts and chocolate, are toxic to dogs.

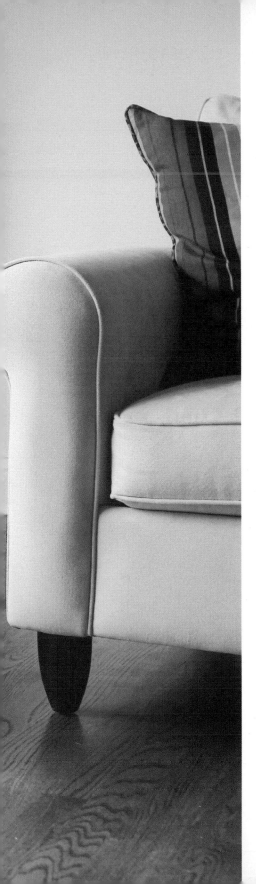

Chapter 5
Crate Training

- Choosing the right crate size and type
- What to put in the crate—and what to keep out
- Teaching the puppy to love the crate

A crate will be one of the most important parts of your puppy's life. It will help you with housetraining, provide a safe place for your puppy to rest, and give you a spot to put your puppy if he gets too rambunctious. Because the crate is so important, it is worth the effort to ensure the puppy always loves his crate.

Some people are hesitant to use a crate because they think it's cruel, and even refer to it as a jail. Nothing could be further from the truth. Crates are not inhumane if they're not used as punishment, and are by far preferable to leaving the puppy loose while you're away from home. A crate can save your puppy's life by keeping him out of mischief when you're not with him. It can also save your relationship with the puppy and enable you to keep him rather than relinquish him to a shelter due to bad behavior.

People often complain that their puppy is ruining their lives because he's destructive and makes messes all over the house. Often the owner is at the point of finding a new home for the dog. But if a trainer recommends a crate, many dog owners get upset and say they could never put the puppy in a "cage." Parents put toddlers and babies into playpens for safety, and that's what you are doing with the puppy. It doesn't mean he will have to use his crate forever, but it is important that he like it from the beginning.

Good crate behavior will also come in handy if you travel with your dog. Most hotels require that the dog be contained while you are not with him. If you take your puppy to visit friends and family, he may need to be in a crate to be a good houseguest.

Crates also keep puppies safe while traveling in a vehicle. A puppy climbing on a driver is dangerous. And in the event of an accident, a crate may keep the puppy from being hurt or killed.

Choosing a Crate

There are many different types of crates, but most people use wire or plastic versions. For the fashion conscious, you can even get crates that resemble fine pieces of furniture. Most crates start in the $50 range and rapidly go up depending on material and size. However, more affordable used crates are often available in classified ads. Also check with a local animal rescue or shelter to see if they sell gently used crates.

For housetraining purposes, the crate should be just large enough for the puppy to stand up and turn around. Dogs generally don't like to potty in the same place where they sleep. If the crate is too large, the puppy will have room to make part of it his toilet. Once the puppy is housebroken, you can give him a larger crate so he can stretch out.

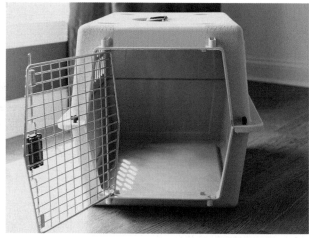

Wire Crates

For some people the wire crates may be more advantageous, as many of them come with a divider that allows you to make the living space larger or smaller. This way you can get a crate that will be large enough for when your puppy grows up, but which you can still divide into a smaller area for housetraining purposes. If you go this route, make sure you purchase the type that comes with the divider, as not all wire crates offer this feature. Most wire crates also easily fold up, making them perfect for travel. Wire crates also generally come with a removable plastic floor liner, which makes cleaning easier.

Plastic Kennels

Plastic kennels can provide more of a "den-like" atmosphere, and some dogs prefer that to the openness of the wire crates. Some plastic crates come apart easily, but others do not. Keep that in mind if you will need to take the crate apart often. This type of crate works best if you're leaving it in place and don't need to move it around. Plastic crates generally do not have a divider or removable floor pan.

Never use your puppy's crate as punishment. You want him to always think of his crate as the happiest place on Earth. If you force your puppy into the crate or yell at him and then put him in his crate, it will become a place to be feared. You can use the crate as a timeout if the puppy needs a place to chill, but he still has to think it is fun to go into his crate. Use your happy voice and give your puppy a reward for going in his crate, and he will never know you're putting him there because he has gotten on your very last nerve.

For housetraining purposes, the crate should be just large enough for the puppy to stand up and turn around.

What Should Be in the Puppy's Crate?

Often, what we choose to put in the puppy's crate is more of a reflection of what humans think would be comfortable. Putting in a comfy bed may be fine for some puppies, but it may provide hours of playing "tear up the bed" for others. When choosing something new to put in the puppy's crate, always do so on a day when you'll be home so you can monitor what happens. You don't want him to chew up his bedding and swallow some of the material, which could lead to a life-threatening event. Toys can also cause issues if they are the type the puppy can chew up, as he might end up swallowing large chunks of indigestible material.

If your puppy can't be trusted to not chew up bedding, consider something like thick rubber matting. Many pet stores also sell specific crate bedding that is designed to be more difficult to chew up.

Puppies do need something in their crates for entertainment. Good options are long-lasting chews that are designed to be eaten, such as bully sticks or elk antlers. A hollow rubber food-dispensing toy is also a great option.

Things That Should Not Be in the Crate

Do not put your puppy's water bowl in the crate unless it's recommended by your veterinarian. Most puppies end up knocking the bowl over and making a mess. If the puppy is too young for good bladder control, the extra water will cause accidents. Also, consider taking your puppy's collar off before he goes into his crate. A collar or tags could become caught in the bars and present a choking hazard.

During housebreaking, using blankets or other bedding may give the puppy a place to pee and poop that he can then easily move aside to give him a clean place to sleep. It may be more practical to wait until a puppy is completely housebroken before adding bedding to the crate.

Crate Placement

During housetraining, you will need the crate in your bedroom or at least close enough so you can hear your puppy if he starts crying to go outside during the night. The crate should not be near heating or cooling vents and should be placed in an area free from drafts. Crates should be in areas that can be made off-limits to children and other pets to ensure your puppy is not bothered when he is resting. You may wish to have two or more crates so he can be near you when you are in a family room as well as when you are sleeping.

Training the Puppy to Go into His Crate

Set up the crate in a room where you spend a lot of time. You're going to be here a while, so you might as well be comfortable. Find treats your puppy really loves but doesn't get often, such as meat or cheese. You need treats that are so tasty your puppy will really want to win them. Place the crate facing you with the door blocked open in a position that will allow you to toss treats into it. You want to make sure the door stays open and doesn't accidentally swing shut and scare the puppy.

Sit quietly and stare at the crate as if it is totally fascinating. If the puppy moves toward the crate, praise him and place some treats near the door. When he goes near the door, toss some treats just inside. If he appears happy to be near the crate, toss treats farther into it. If he is hesitant to go in, stop tossing treats inside and just put them near the door until he is comfortable being near the crate.

If the puppy will happily run into the crate after a treat, ask him to come out and then close the door. Wait a few minutes and open the door again and see if he will go in or at least stick his nose inside. If he does, make treats rain from the sky and praise the puppy.

Call the puppy out of the crate and see if he will go back in on his own; if so, repeat the lavish praise and treats. If he isn't going in, go back to tossing in some treats for him to run in and eat.

You want the puppy to think that running into the crate results in lots of treats. As he figures out that going into the crate equals reward, give this game a name such as "crate," "kennel," or whatever makes sense. Always use that word when you ask your puppy to go into his crate.

Once the puppy is happily running into the crate, calmly close the door while he's in. Ignore him by turning your back or looking away for a few seconds.

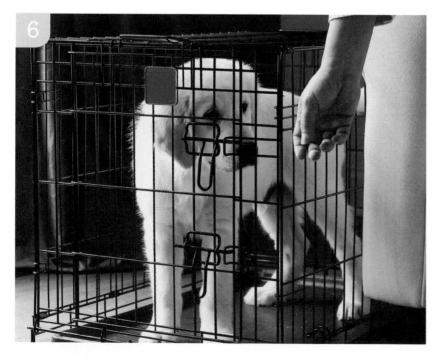

Immediately open the door and give the puppy a treat. Ask him to come out of the crate. If he is crying, whining, or scratching at the door, you probably left it closed too long. Wait for him to calm down (even if it's just for a moment) before opening the door.

Next begin shutting the door and leaving the puppy in the crate. Give him something fun to chew, such as a food-dispensing toy filled with yummy treats. This will only be given when he is inside the crate and the door is closed. If the door is open, the high-value item goes away. He will quickly learn that if he wants this great thing to chew on, it only appears when he is in the crate and the door is closed.

Leave the room when the puppy is in the crate. Wait until he is fully engaged in chewing on whatever you have left for him, and walk away. When you come back, drop some treats in the crate. Don't be too predictable. While your goal is to teach him to stay in the crate for longer periods of time, you don't want him to think that every time he goes in, the door will close or you will be gone for a longer period. Gradually increase the time he's in the crate, but mix it up with times when he isn't in for very long.

Crate Training Tips and Troubleshooting

Do not let your puppy out of the crate if he is whining, barking, or scratching at the door. Wait for him to have all four feet on the floor or to be back away from the door before you open it. If he is barking nonstop, wait for him to take a breath or for a bark that isn't quite as loud, then give him a treat. After he eats the treat, if there are a few seconds of quiet, open the crate door.

It's not unusual for puppies to cry and whine when they're in the crate for the first time. Avoid the urge to talk to them or go to them. Most puppies will settle down and begin to chew on whatever you have left for them. If you get in the habit of talking to your puppy while he's barking or whining in his crate, or if you constantly go check on him, he will just bark or whine for longer and longer periods in an effort to make you come back.

If he is extremely agitated to the point that he's injuring himself trying to get out of the crate, let him out and consult a professional trainer.

Getting More Creative

If the puppy won't settle down and chew on whatever you have left for him in the crate, experiment and look for things he really wants. Just because you think something looks fun to chew on doesn't mean your puppy will love it.

Don't become a creature of habit when it comes to crate training. Many people only put their puppies in the crate at night or when they leave for work. Puppies are smart and will figure out this pattern, and they may start to become anxious in the moments before you ask them to go into the crate. Your puppy should learn to be crated both when you are home and when you leave for work. That way he won't think that the only time he stays in the crate is when you leave for the day.

Crate your puppy at different times during the day, so he never knows when he might be going into the crate. Leave him in the crate for varying amounts of time. You never want the puppy to know if he will be in the crate for three minutes or three hours.

Make It Rewarding

The trick to successful crate training is to make the crate fun, to always have something great to chew on as soon as the puppy goes in, and to vary the amount of time he spends in the crate.

Always give the dog a treat for going in the crate. A great crate behavior will be important throughout your dog's life, so this is one place where you always want to give him a nice reward.

Troubleshooting

If your puppy is terrified of the crate, chances are someone has forced him into a crate and he had a bad experience. You might be able to retrain the behavior by simply getting a different kind of crate. For example, if you know he had a bad experience in a wire crate, get a plastic crate instead and go back to step 1 of crate training.

If your puppy is worried about the crate, you could also consider blocking the door open and feeding him in the crate for several days. If he is too scared to go into the crate, just place his food bowl near the opening and gradually move the food inside the crate as he gets used to it.

Clicker Training for the Crate

You can shape the puppy's behavior to make him comfortable going into the crate by using a clicker. Stand by the crate with the door open and stare into the crate. When your puppy comes to investigate this thing that has captured your attention, click and treat (C/T). Then begin to click and treat any time he looks at the door of the crate. As he begins to understand it's looking at the crate that is earning the click and treat, ask for more. Wait for the puppy to stick his nose into the opening before you C/T. From there you just begin to ask him to put more of his body in the crate and C/T each time he responds.

Once he is happily going in and out of the crate, refer to the previous training steps.

Chapter 6

Housetraining

- What to do before you start housetraining
- Steps for successful potty training
- Advanced housetraining

Housebreaking is one of the biggest issues pet parents have. When pets are taken to animal shelters, incomplete housetraining is one of the reasons most often listed as why the animal is being surrendered.

Housebreaking is possible with any breed. Many people make excuses for why a dog is not housebroken, citing breed, stubbornness, dominating behavior, etc. In reality, dogs are not housebroken because people are not consistent or don't do a good job of teaching the dog from the beginning. However, the longer you allow housebreaking issues to go on, the longer they will take to fix later. It is far better to get started on the right foot with something this important.

Potty training is really simple, but it does take consistency and patience. You reward the puppy when he goes where you want him to and ignore him if he has an accident. You have to watch the puppy constantly until he is reliably housebroken, which means keeping him with you all the time or putting him in a crate. Most housebreaking issues happen because owners do not keep a close eye on the puppy. Be vigilant at all times!

Young puppies do not have the ability to control their bowel and bladder for long periods of time. If your puppy is between 8 and 12 weeks of age, expect to take him out every hour or two during the day. You will probably need to get up at least once or twice during the night for puppies this young. Once most dogs reach 12 weeks of age, they can often go three to four hours without an accident during the day and may be able to go all night without needing out. Most puppies will be able to control their bowel and bladder for eight hours by the time they are 6 months of age.

Just remember, these are only general guidelines. Every puppy will be different, just as children are not all potty trained at the same age or with the same degree of ease.

Before You Start Housetraining

Here are some things to consider before you get started with housetraining.

Where to Go?

Most people eventually want their dog to eliminate outdoors. If that is your goal, it is better to start taking the puppy outside to potty from the beginning rather than first teaching him to go inside on potty pads or paper. Otherwise, housebreaking takes longer, and some puppies have a hard time figuring out it is no longer okay to go inside.

If you live in an apartment or other place where getting outside quickly is difficult, you may want to use potty pads, artificial turf, or a doggy litter box. Consider these options also if you must leave your puppy alone for hours before he is old enough to have good control of his bodily functions. Many potty pads are scented to attract puppies to eliminate on them, which makes them a better option than newspaper.

Whether you are teaching the puppy to go outside or on a special surface inside, make sure everyone in the family knows the designated spot and keeps the route to that place free from obstacles. You will often need to get there fast.

Supervision

Puppies do not like to pee or poop where they sleep. In order to effectively housetrain your puppy, you need a place to put him when you are unable to watch him. This place needs to be small enough so the puppy would have to lie in his mess if he went to the bathroom. A crate is the best option for effective housetraining. (See Chapter 5 on crate training before you begin housetraining.) The crate should be small enough that the puppy can only stand up and turn around. Don't put in bedding until after your puppy is housebroken. Puppies often pee or poop in the bedding and then move it to one side so they have a clean place to sleep.

Successful housetraining requires 100 percent supervision. If you can't watch the puppy, he needs to be in his crate. Puppies are notorious for wandering off and pottying when your back is turned. Consider attaching him to you by a leash hooked to your belt to ensure he stays with you. Another option is to use baby gates to keep him in a room with you to make watching him easier.

Puppies generally need to potty as soon as they come out of their crate after napping, after they eat, and after they play. These are always times to be especially vigilant and get your puppy to his designated area.

Accidents Will Happen

Be prepared for accidents. No matter how vigilant you are, the puppy will have an accident. You can use specially formulated cleaners, designed to eliminate most of the urine or feces odor, to clean up messes. Block access to any rooms with floor coverings that will be difficult to clean. Puppies often pick places to go where they can smell that they went before. You can clean up the mess with a good enzymatic cleaner so no odor is left behind.

Treats for Housetraining Success

Use a high-value treat that your puppy does not get often, such as hot dogs or boiled chicken. The treat must be something truly tasty so the puppy really wants to get it. This will be a special treat the puppy gets whenever he potties in his designated area.

First Steps to Potty Training Your Puppy

Take your puppy to his designated spot on a leash. If he potties in the proper place, immediately say "good dog" and give him a high-value treat. Dogs have a very short association window, so you have only a few seconds to give him a treat for him to understand he is getting it for going potty. Don't interrupt the puppy as he potties, but the praise and treat must come immediately after.

When the puppy is doing his business in an appropriate spot, give him a cue such as "hurry up" or "go potty." That way, when you are in a new environment or when you need him to know that now is the time to go, he will understand that the cue means this is the place to potty.

Do not let your puppy loose in a fenced yard when you are training. He must be on leash so you can be right beside him. Often people watch from a doorway and reward the puppy after he comes back in the house. This rewards him for coming in, not for pottying outside. Only let your puppy off his leash to play after he goes to the bathroom. This will also teach him that the faster he does his business, the sooner he can play.

If the puppy does not potty within a few minutes while you have him at his potty spot, put him back in his crate or keep him at your side so you can watch him. Wait five minutes and take him to the spot again. Repeat this process until the puppy does potty either outside or on the designated surface inside. Then have a huge party with lots of praise and treats.

If you are teaching your puppy to eliminate outdoors, avoid making him go back in the house the minute he potties. Puppies who are taught to go back in right after pottying sometimes hold their bodily functions longer hoping for more outside time. The same can happen if you take your puppy for a walk and immediately head for home the minute he does his business. The puppy may learn that if he wants to go for a longer walk, he just has to hold off pottying for longer.

Do not leave the puppy in a crate if you are going to be gone longer than he can comfortably hold his bowel or bladder. If you have to be gone more than a few hours when the puppy is young, set up a small pen for him. The pen should be just large enough for a bed or his crate and the potty pads or doggy litter box. This will give him a place to potty and also a clean place to rest.

Advanced Potty Training

If you start out using potty pads indoors, but eventually want your puppy to go outdoors, begin transitioning him by placing the potty pads outside in the area you want him to go. Follow all of the preceding steps, taking him out on leash and praising him as soon as he potties in the new spot. Block access to the area where he was going in the house so that he won't be tempted to go back to the same spot.

Once he is going outdoors on the potty pads without issue, make the pads smaller. Eventually they will be so small, the puppy will be going mostly on the ground. At this point you can take away the potty pads.

Going in Other Places

In the beginning, always taking your puppy to the same spot will help him understand that is where he should go. However, once your puppy understands the cue you have taught him that means this is the place to go, vary the routine and start asking him to go in other places. If he learns to go only in one place or only at certain times, you may have issues when you travel with him or when your schedule changes. Schedules are important when you are first housetraining, but later you want the puppy to be able to eliminate at different times of the day so if you need to change your routine he won't be confused.

Once your puppy is reliably holding his bowel and bladder, you can begin to give him more freedom in the house. At first only let him roam one or two rooms. Pick the rooms where any accidents will be easiest to clean up. There is no magic formula you can use to know when your puppy is ready for more freedom. Start by leaving him alone for just 15 minutes or so and gradually work up to more and more time. If he has an accident, go back a few steps in your training.

Signaling When They Need to Go

Many dogs will signal when they need to go. Dogs that are trained to go outdoors will often sniff near the door when they want to potty. Or they will begin sniffing in circles when they are looking for a spot. If you see this behavior, hurry and take your dog to his designated area. Soon he will learn that by exhibiting this behavior in front of you, you will take him outside to eliminate.

However, most dogs learn to just hold their bodily functions until you let them outside. As long as you are consistent in letting the dog out and don't make him wait longer than his body can handle, he will learn to wait for an opportunity to go outside.

What to Do If He Has an Accident

Never punish a puppy for peeing or pooping in the house. Ignore all potty accidents. If you yell at him, he will learn to hide from you when he needs to potty. Pet parents often take this as a sign that the puppy "knows" he is "bad" to potty inside, when in reality, hiding from you is what the puppy assumes you want. If you yell at him for peeing or pooping in front of you, he will think you don't like that, so you must want him to potty where you can't see him.

Never rub your puppy's nose in pee or poop. This will just cause stress and it could cause your puppy to struggle or try to bite you.

If you see your puppy about to pee or poop, you can try distracting him with your voice (use a happy voice, not an angry voice) and then immediately pick him up and carry him to his designated spot.

If the puppy keeps going in the same spot no matter how well you clean it, find a way to block access to that place. Sometimes a puppy will remember he went in a certain spot, and simply stopping him from getting to that spot will help teach him you want him pottying elsewhere.

If your puppy continues to have accidents no matter what you do, consult your veterinarian. Some medical conditions can cause dogs to have accidents. Stress also causes housebreaking issues. Owners often find their dogs pottying in the house after moving, or after adding another person or pet to the household. If this happens, you may need to just go back to beginning housetraining, keep the dog crated more often, and reward him for going in the right spot.

Puppies that come from puppy mills often are harder to housetrain because they were raised in a space that did not allow them to eliminate away from where they slept. If you purchased a dog you suspect came from a puppy mill and have issues housebreaking, consult a professional trainer as soon as possible.

Chapter 7

Socialization

- Stress: signs and triggers
- Human vs. dog body language
- Places to socialize

Socialization is the most important thing you can do to ensure a good life for your puppy. A properly socialized dog will be confident in public meeting new people and other animals. A dog without proper socialization may grow up to be afraid of strangers and things like bicycles. Many serious issues people have with adolescent or adult dogs can be traced back to improper socialization when the dog was a puppy.

Between the ages of 3 weeks and 3 months, puppies are like sponges. They soak up new experiences and file them away as good or bad. This is the socialization period. After this period ends, puppies tend to view anything new as possibly dangerous. The more places your puppy visits and the more people she meets during this period, the more likely she will grow up not being afraid in similar situations. However, all the experiences she has during this period must be fun. If she gets scared of something during this time, she may be afraid of it her entire life.

If you are lucky enough to get your puppy between 8 and 12 weeks old, you have four weeks during which to expose her to new stimuli. If you purchased her from a responsible breeder, that breeder likely will also have been working on socialization between 3 and 8 weeks. The period between 12 and 16 weeks may still be in that socialization window, but during that time the puppy may start to see new things as dangerous.

Don't despair if your puppy is already older than 3 months. Depending on what happened to her during those first three months and the time and expertise you bring to the relationship, things will still turn out just fine.

The trick to socializing a puppy is to go slow and work at the pace of the puppy. You need to understand the signs of stress and then become a body language detective to ensure she is having as much fun as you think.

Signs of Stress

Canines communicate via body language. Understanding some of that body language can help you know when your puppy is worried. The first step is to know exactly what your puppy looks like when she is relaxed. Where does she carry her tail and her ears? Does she naturally have any white showing around her eyes? What does her forehead look like when she is relaxed? If you know how she looks when relaxed, then you will know when she starts to get stressed.

Some of the signals we will talk about are *displacement gestures,* meaning something the dog does naturally (like sniffing), but is out of context to the situation. Other signals are *appeasement gestures,* which are signals the dog uses to tell whatever is making her nervous that she means no harm. In order to simplify things, just think of the following as signs your dog may need more space or is becoming nervous.

If you become proficient at reading these signals, your dog will never need to get to a growl or a bite in order to tell you she is worried. If you ignore these signals and the dog continues to feel frightened, she may feel the need to show her teeth, growl, or bite.

Signs from the Head

The dog's head can tell you a lot. Watch for yawning or lip licking, and for white around the dog's eyes. Unlike humans, most dogs do not naturally show any white around their eyes. When they do, it is referred to as a "whale eye" and it means the dog is looking at you from the corner of her eye but is trying not to make direct eye contact. If a dog turns her head away from someone or something approaching, she also may be saying, "I don't see you; go away."

A dog approached by a child will often turn her head away from the child. The dog thinks she is clearly saying "stay away." So when the child ignores that signal and rushes up to hug the dog, the dog may be overwhelmed and feel threatened because the signal to back off was not heeded.

A dog that is worried may have more wrinkling on her forehead than normal. The dog may pant more or faster than exertion or heat would indicate as normal. A worried dog may have very dilated pupils. If the dog flattens her ears back, she may be trying to say she means no harm to whatever is making her nervous.

Signs from the Tail

The tail is also very expressive, but don't be fooled by a wagging tail. People often assume that a dog wagging his tail is friendly. All a tail wag really means is that the dog is ready for action. That action could be to launch himself into a fight. If the dog's entire body is wagging with the tail, that is generally friendly, but if just the tail is wagging, the dog may be signaling his intent to do something, such as charge forward.

Most people recognize if a dog tucks his tail down over his butt or between his legs that he is scared. A dog may also flag his tail up very high over his back, which could be telling another dog or a person to back off.

A dog that is worried or stressed may pant heavily, yawn, or lick nervously. Ears that are flat or set back are another sign that the dog is uncomfortable in a situation.

Other Signs of Stress

Dogs that are stressed will often sniff something on the ground near them excessively, or they will sniff or lick their genitalia. A stressed dog may shake as if he just came out of a bath, or suddenly scratch as if he has a serious itch.

A dog that is extremely stressed won't eat. So if your dog is very food motivated and she suddenly stops taking treats, she may be very worried about something. However, just because a dog does eat doesn't mean she is totally fine with a situation. High-value treats may entice a dog to eat even though she is really worried.

One thing to keep in mind is that just because a dog does show some of these signs doesn't always mean she is stressed. A dog might yawn because she is tired or scratch because she has an itch. However, if you see these signs in a close sequence, or if people or other dogs are coming closer to your dog, pay attention. Be prepared to remove your dog from the situation or ask the person coming closer to stop and turn away.

Ways to Lessen the Fear

Be especially vigilant if your dog is on a leash or in a small space with no escape routes. A dog that can move away from a scary or stressful situation will usually do so. But a dog on a leash or trapped in a corner has no good options if she gets stressed.

Many people worry that giving their dog a treat if he is scared is rewarding the dog for being afraid. Fear is something the dog can't control. You can, however, change a dog's response to the fearsome object. If a dog is terrified of something and you can get him to turn away from it and eat a high-value treat, he may gradually become more interested in eating the food and feel less scared. You have changed the dog's response to the feared object.

If a dog is afraid of thunder or other loud noises, act like the noises mean nothing to you. Remain calm and see if you can change the situation by moving the dog to a location farther away from the object or noise. Often people become concerned if a dog shows a fearful response. The owner may coddle the dog or make a big deal out of the scary noise or object. This makes the dog even more nervous. You always want to show the dog that whatever it is doesn't bother you.

If your puppy becomes stressed while working on socialization, work at the puppy's pace and increase both the value of the treats and the distance from the scary object.

Puppy Body Language

To help your puppy become socialized, it is important to understand some differences between human body language and canine body language.

Eye Contact and Body Contact

Humans make direct eye contact with each other; they stand in front of other people. People may hug a friend or shake hands with an acquaintance. These are friendly gestures between two humans, but they could be considered threats if you did the same things to a dog.

Direct eye contact between two dogs can be a threat. Petting some dogs on top of the head or on top of the neck can be stressful to the dog. Many dogs actually hate being hugged or having a person put his or her face right in the dog's face. Because we are taller than dogs, we bend over to pet them, often placing our body so it looms over the dog's body. This can be terribly stressful to many dogs.

Luckily, our own dogs tend to figure out over time that these rude (in terms of canine body language) gestures are not meant as a threat. However, many dogs are never comfortable with these gestures, and some will be especially fearful of strangers petting them on top of the head or standing over them.

How to Behave When Meeting a Dog

When meeting a dog, avoid direct eye contact. Just watch the dog from the corner of your eye. Keep your body loose and turned slightly to the side of the dog. Puppies are very small, so get down on their level instead of bending over them. Although your puppy is adorable, avoid the urge to hug it or carry it around like a baby.

When meeting a new person, if the pup is nervous, notice whether the person is doing something that the puppy might consider disturbing or a threat. Then ask the person to kneel down, avoid direct eye contact, or stop petting the puppy on top of the head, if that is the issue.

Instead of petting your puppy on top of the head, try scratching her under the chin or rubbing her chest.

Learning to Like Being Petted on the Head

While it may be rude to pet a dog on top of the head, humans will do it anyway, so it is better to teach your puppy to be happy with the gesture rather than try to change the humans around the puppy. Here's how:

1. Give your dog some treats, and while she eats out of your hand, gently pet the top of her head.

2. If she continues eating, keep petting her.

3. If she flinches, backs up, or stops eating, stop and see if you can pet her on the back or sides instead while she eats, and gradually work your way up to her head.

Is Your Puppy Having Fun?

The key to proper socialization is to ensure the puppy is always having fun. Forcing a puppy to face something scary isn't the answer. Everything has to go at the puppy's pace.

If you aren't sure if your puppy is having fun during an activity, stop and watch her. Does she obviously want to leave the area? If so, she may be getting stressed and you should consider leaving the situation or moving farther away until the puppy relaxes. If she seems momentarily concerned but after a few minutes relaxes, give her some time to acclimate before asking her for more interest in the scary object.

A key to socialization is to not be afraid to stop whatever you are doing and leave if you realize your puppy is not having as much fun as you are.

How to Make a Scary Object Fun

1. Many dogs are terrified of statues of people or animals. Proper socialization would be to start far away from the statue and watch the puppy's body language. If she appears to see the statue but is totally uninterested, you want to stop and give her some treats. Let her look at the statue from a distance and reward her for just looking in the direction of the statue. If you are using a clicker to train with, you should click and treat each time she looks at the statue.

2. Next you would wait for the puppy to move closer to the statue on her own. Even if she just takes a tiny step forward, she should get lots of treats for being so brave. As long as you go slow and let the puppy decide how close to get to the statue, she will soon learn that moving closer results in awesome treats.

3. If she stops moving forward or shows signs of stress, stop and perhaps take a step back. Talk to her, give her some chin scratches, and if she looks at the statue again, give her lots of praise and treats.

Do not use the treats to lure the puppy closer to the statue. The allure of food can overcome the puppy's fear, but that doesn't mean she is having fun. She just wants to get the food and get out quickly. If she gets up to the statue and the food runs out and she suddenly panics, she may decide following treats leads to danger. And you may have a pup that will never go near statues.

Go slow and work at the puppy's pace. It may take you hours, days, or more than a week to get the puppy close to the statue. But if you let her make the choices, she will learn to trust you and decide new experiences can be fun.

Places to Socialize Your Puppy

A good way to socialize a puppy is to have her experience something new three to five times a week. It might be meeting a new person, walking on a new surface, or visiting a new place. The more novel experiences your puppy can have that are fun and not scary, the more confident she will be as an adult. Be sure to read Chapter 10 before you take your pup new places in a vehicle. Car rides can be scary, so you want to train the puppy to love the car.

People often wait to take their puppy out in public or introduce her to other dogs or puppies until she is 4 or 5 months old and has received all of her vaccinations. This is something you should discuss with your veterinarian. It won't do any good to protect your puppy from disease if she grows up to be a dog you can't take out in public due to a behavior issue.

Also consider taking your puppy to classes as soon as possible. Many people wait for classes until a puppy is older or is causing them headaches. It is far better to go to class before you have issues. A good trainer running a proper puppy class can keep you on the right path for a well-adjusted adult dog.

Taking your puppy out in public has many similarities to taking a baby out. Depending on your plans, you may wish to pack long-lasting chew snacks, poop bags, lots of high-value treats, toys, water, and possibly even a towel for your puppy's comfort. Don't be so set on a schedule that you can't make adjustments. If your plan was to take the puppy on a shopping trip but you discover once you reach the store that she is terrified or just plain having a bad day, be prepared to not shop and just go back home rather than force her to accommodate your schedule.

The key to good socialization is just to go slow and always have fun. Do not take your puppy to visit every friend or relative you have the first day your puppy arrives home. You also don't want to make your puppy's first outing with you a trip to the local pet store. A visit to the pet store should actually be one of the last things on your socialization list, as pet stores can be overwhelming.

Meeting People

Your puppy needs to meet people of all races, sizes, and ages. The more different types of people you can introduce her to, the less likely she will grow up to be afraid of new people she meets. The important thing is variety. Even if you don't have children, your puppy should still meet as many kids of various ages as possible. Make sure she meets people wearing puffy coats, sunglasses, and hats as well. These things make the person look different to the pup, and different can be scary.

Start your human socialization with a friend. Discuss the differences between human and canine communication so you set up your friend and the puppy for success.

Your friend should crouch down several feet from the puppy. If the puppy is wiggly and goes forward to the stranger, have your friend offer her a treat. If the puppy is having fun, the friend should continue to interact, petting and talking to her.

If the puppy barks, backs up, or appears stressed, ask your friend to move back to a distance where the puppy seems less agitated.

Have the person toss treats to the puppy. If the puppy is nervous, always let her decide to move toward the stranger rather than having the stranger move toward her. Avoid luring the puppy closer with food. The food should be tossed to her so she can get it without coming closer than she is comfortable.

Now you have a baseline for what your puppy thinks about new people. If she is having fun, it is time to meet more people. The great thing about socializing puppies to people is that you don't have to do much work in terms of finding people. Take your pup to any public place that allows dogs, and chances are good people will flock to you for a chance to interact with the puppy.

Ask people you meet on a walk if they would like to give your puppy a treat. Soon your puppy will learn that meeting new people is an opportunity to get a treat. As your pup's confidence grows, you can add more people to the group. Just always be prepared to ask people to give the puppy space if she starts to get nervous.

New Places

It is important that your puppy visit many new places. Often new owners only take the puppy to the vet or to training. Both of these can be stressful destinations. You want to make sure your puppy thinks that getting in the car could lead to fun.

Going to the bank? Take the puppy. When you get to the bank, take the puppy out of the vehicle, walk her around the parking lot, give her a couple of great treats, get back in the car, and go through the drive-through. Give the puppy treats while you are talking to the teller, as many dogs react negatively to hearing voices come out of speaker boxes. If she is calm and relaxed while you talk, praise her and give her treats. If she appears stressed by the talking box, make treats rain from the sky.

Most large stores have huge parking lots with the activity centered close to the entrance. Take your puppy to the store, but park far away from the entrance in a quiet corner of the parking lot. Take her for a little walk around the car, and let her see the people in the distance and hear the sound of shopping carts. Give her some treats while she walks around. Stay less than five minutes, get back in the car, and drive to a new parking lot and repeat the game. As the puppy becomes more confident, park closer to the activity and let her gradually acclimate to more hustle and bustle.

Outdoor shopping centers can be an awesome training ground. Start during a time when few shoppers will be about. Scout out the area first and hide some treats along your path, especially in areas where the puppy might be cautious. Large windows that could show reflections are an option, as reflections can be scary to the pup. As you walk her, help her figure out that she needs to look for the treats. Soon she will decide that exploring new locations can be fun.

Wait to take your pup to the many pet-friendly stores until she already has some skills under her belt and you are confident in your ability to read her body language. It is not uncommon to encounter dogs and people in the stores who are lacking proper doggie etiquette. Be prepared to cut the outing short if the store is crowded or you encounter owners who allow their dogs to rush in and overwhelm your pup. Your first trip should be about entering and exiting the building and having fun. Don't try to actually do any shopping.

Many pet stores have automatic doors, which can absolutely terrify a puppy. Stand well away from the doors and just let your pup see them open and close, and watch a few dogs enter and exit before taking her toward the entrance. Don't force the puppy to go through the doors. Wait for her to feel confident about going through on her own.

Once she is comfortable entering and exiting the store, begin staying longer. Take a friend along who can grab a shopping cart and get the puppy used to walking near a cart. If the pet store sells reptiles, birds, or fish, use that opportunity to let your puppy see them. However, please be respectful of these other creatures. Your puppy should not be allowed to terrorize the small animals on display. Instead, teach her to ignore those fun things and win a great reward from you instead.

Other Surfaces and Heights

Puppies should be exposed to many different surfaces, such as laminate or hardwood floors. You also want to know that your puppy can go up and down different types of steps with ease. Think about what your future life with the puppy will look like and what kinds of places she may need to be exposed to.

Learning to Walk on a New Surface

1. If your puppy is afraid to walk on certain types of surfaces, sit just inside the doorway between a surface she is comfortable with and the one she is afraid of. Put her on a long leash so she has plenty of room and won't feel as if she is being forced onto the flooring.

2. Most puppies will try to walk on a new surface if you just give them time. You might sit quietly and read a book and watch her. If she ventures onto the surface, give her a treat. Once she figures out how to place her feet, she will become more confident.

If you have another dog that isn't afraid of that surface, take it into the room and let the puppy see the other dog walking on the flooring. Once she realizes the floor doesn't eat puppies, she may give it a try. Avoid throwing toys onto slick floors so the pup doesn't slip and fall while chasing something.

When you are on a walk, you may also encounter a surface that is new to the puppy. Avoid the temptation to force her to continue the walk. In the beginning you should always have treats with you so you can reward your puppy for being brave and trying new things.

Learning to Walk on Stairs

Stairs can be especially scary. Begin working on steps that are closed and that the puppy cannot see through. Carpeted stairways will be easier to navigate as well.

1. Sit a few steps up with the puppy on a long leash so she has plenty of room. Again you may wish to read a book and wait for her to figure out how to navigate the steps.

2. If she puts her front feet on the bottom step, have a big treat party.

3. Put a treat on the edge of the second step to see if she will try pulling her back feet onto the first step.

4. Once she figures out how to get onto a step, put treats on each step so she has to keep her head down and watch the steps carefully. Teach her to go up and down the steps safely.

Playgrounds and Parks

Playgrounds and parks can be awesome places to take your puppy for socialization. In the beginning, choose days or times of the day when the park will be less crowded.

Take your puppy on a walk and see if she encounters objects that appear to make her nervous. Rocks can often be scary to puppies. Go back to the technique for working with a statue for any new object the puppy seems afraid of.

If you find objects that are steady and that the puppy might be able to put her front feet on, begin to encourage her to do so. Teach your puppy how to target your hand (see Chapter 10) and ask her to target so that she has to reach up and over the top of an object. If she is having fun, increase the difficulty of the target so she will have to put her front feet up to target the hand. Begin with low objects that would be easy for her to jump onto. Once dogs learn how to jump onto objects, it becomes a fun game. Many dogs enjoy jumping onto logs, rocks, and other objects found in parks.

Playgrounds often have many different surfaces to walk on as well as objects that might be scary to the puppy. They are wonderful training opportunities. Don't try to get the puppy on all of the equipment in the playground on her first visit. Find something easy, such as teaching her to put her front feet on the first step of a ladder up a slide.

If there are children on the playground, this is an awesome opportunity to also introduce your pup to kids. If the children's parents are amenable, you can ask the kids to sit in a circle with treats and each child can give the puppy a treat if the puppy comes up to him or her. Always ask children to hold their palms flat with the treat in the middle so the puppy licks it off rather than possibly nipping fingers if the child holds the treat.

As long as the puppy is having fun, you can then hold the treats yourself and as she eats the treats, ask the children to pet the puppy gently on her back or under her chin. This way the puppy will learn that being petted by kids is fun. Always control your puppy's head just to ensure a safe interaction. You want to be feeding the puppy the entire time kids are petting her so she continues to have fun. Keep sessions short so she doesn't get overwhelmed.

Bicycles, skateboards, and similar objects can also be scary the first time the puppy encounters them. Find a park popular with skaters or bicyclists and let the pup watch from a distance. Gradually get closer to the action, rewarding the puppy for calm behavior. If you notice signs of stress, increase the distance and the treats until the puppy seems interested in moving forward again.

Meeting Other Dogs on Walks

Some dogs are social butterflies and want to meet every dog they see. However, many dogs actually do not enjoy meeting others when going for a walk. When dogs are on leash, it forces them to meet each other face to face, which can be stressful in terms of canine body language. The leashes also prevent dogs from getting away if they become stressed. Some dogs may seem fine going up to meet another dog, but then become scared once they realize how close they are and that they can't get away. This could lead to the dogs growling or snapping at each other.

If your puppy continually meets dogs on a walk and becomes more and more stressed, she may quickly decide that going for a walk is scary. Often dogs will begin barking at other dogs in the distance in order to warn them away. If that doesn't work, the dog could become more and more agitated until it is lunging, growling, or snapping at other dogs.

Dogs do best if they can meet each other in an area where they can control the distance. If you must let your dog meet another dog while both are on leash, keep your leash as loose as possible and make sure the dogs can easily back away from each other.

Even if your puppy enjoys meeting other dogs, the dog she is meeting may not be so eager. You don't want your puppy to think that every time she sees a dog on a walk she will get to meet it. Otherwise as she grows she may begin to drag you toward every dog she sees.

It may be better to teach your pup that when she is on leash and you are on a walk, she won't be going up to sniff other dogs she meets. That way she will grow up ignoring other dogs she sees whenever she is walking on leash. If you want your dog to socialize with other dogs, choose a dog park or doggie day care, or meet up with friends in locations where your dogs can interact off leash.

Chapter 8

Grooming

- Grooming tools you will need
- Bathing, brushing, nail trimming, and other puppy maintenance
- How to choose a professional groomer

Keeping your puppy clean and well groomed is important for his health and well-being. Starting a program of regular grooming when you bring your puppy home is the easiest way to accomplish this. Make grooming a positive part of his routine.

Your puppy's grooming needs will be influenced by a couple of factors. The breed's coat type. Some dogs have short, tight coats, like a German Shorthair Pointer. Others have short but dense coats, like a Labrador Retriever. Double-coated dogs with a thick undercoat like a German Shepherd shed heavily. Dogs with long coats will need grooming to prevent mats. Breeds touted as "nonshedding," such as Poodles, need grooming to prevent mats. Terriers may grow a dry, dull coat that needs to be removed by hand or with a special stripping tool.

With dogs that grow long coats, you may wish to keep them in full or show coat or in a more wash-and-wear version. You have time to decide which you want since your puppy will have a fairly short coat for at least a couple of months. Many families decide on a "puppy coat" type of clip—keeping the hair shorter and easier to care for.

You will also need to decide whether you want to do the grooming yourself or if you will pay a groomer. Many people use a groomer for puppies who require clippers to trim and thin their coats. An occasional bath may be all the grooming you choose to do.

It is important to make grooming time positive for your puppy. Short sessions that include treats can make her look forward to a good brushing. The best way to start is with short sessions. You might want to set a time limit, such as one minute, but gradually build up to five or ten minutes. Find a quiet place to work, and have plenty of tasty treats.

Grooming Tools

What supplies you will need to keep your puppy looking spiffy will vary with his breed and coat type. A good breeder can guide you about any special brushes or grooming advice. Groomers will often share advice if you schedule a "learning visit." Be prepared to pay, but you can gain some valuable tips that will help make your puppy look good with the least amount of effort.

For puppies who will grow a long or double coat, look for a good **pin brush.** This brush has a soft cushion and what look like pins sticking up. You want pins without a bulb at the end. Natural bristle or wood are gentlest, but straight pins work just fine for most dogs.

A **metal comb** with multiple-size teeth is handy.

A short-coated puppy will do well with a **soft-bristle brush** and a **hound glove** (a nubby glove you put on to rub your pup).

A **soft cloth** for wiping around eyes and ears works for all puppies.

For some areas on your pup and some thick but short coats, a **slicker brush** works well. This will have a "T" shape and wire bristles. This may be too harsh for many puppies but can be used at shedding times and on the feathering on the legs and the tail.

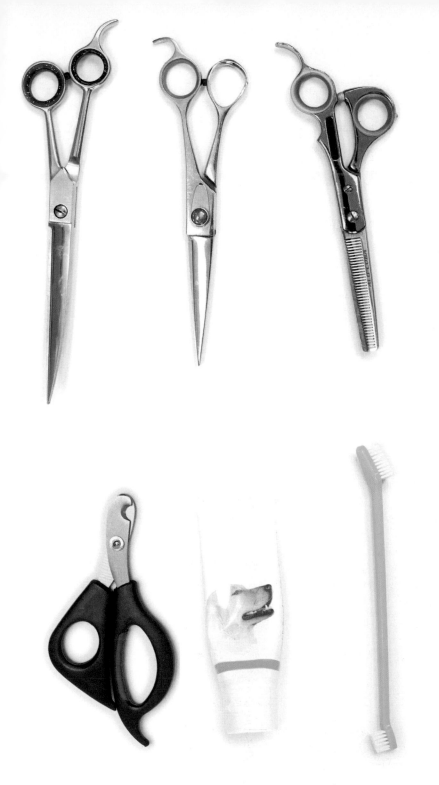

Small **curved scissors** with blunted points are excellent for trimming around the ears, face, and feet.

A regular pair of **hair scissors** can be used for feathering and body trimming.

A set of **thinning shears** is helpful for dogs with thick coats and long feathers.

A soft **chamois towel** helps to dry a puppy quickly.

If you anticipate bathing your own puppy, you may want to invest in a **dog blow dryer.** This will use tepid air rather than hot air, which can damage delicate coat hairs.

There are **mitts** made for wiping your puppy's feet on muddy outings. These can hang on a doorknob so they are handy right when you come in from outside.

You need to trim nails unless you want to schedule regular groomer or vet clinic visits for this task. There are three main nail-trimming tools: a **guillotine nail cutter,** a **scissor-type nail cutter,** and a **rotary grinding** tool. Find out if your pup has had nails done and which method worked well for him.

Don't forget to buy a **doggie toothbrush** or soft children's brush and some **flavored toothpaste** made especially for dogs (never use human toothpaste). Some people are more comfortable with the rubber finger brushes for daily tooth care.

Trimming Nails

Trimming your puppy's nails can be a battle or it can be quick and easy. Make this as positive an experience as possible for your puppy.

Before You Even Trim

Ideally, your puppy will arrive with nails trimmed. That gives you 10 to 14 days to prepare for trimming. Start by holding his paws every day. Do a quick hold and release, followed by a treat. This is easiest to do with him in your lap or on his side on the floor or a grooming table.

After your puppy can handle this, hold each paw a bit longer. Eventually squeeze the paw gently. Touch each toe. He should be relaxed about having his feet handled.

Rub a nail trimmer along the pad and the toes. Give treats if he stays calm. If you use a rotary tool, run it near but not touching your pup's paws. You want him used to the noise.

How Far to Cut?

No one wants to hurt their puppy trimming his nails. Luckily puppies have thin nails with an obvious curve. When you look from the side, you will see the nails have a "hook" at the end. The thicker part of the nail has nerves and blood vessels. You want to remove only the hook.

Some puppies fuss when you actually begin to trim nails. If this happens, do just one or two nails or one foot and stop. You can do more later.

Oh No! Blood!

Trimming a nail too short can happen. Don't panic! Your puppy may squeal for a second. Grab a silver nitrate pencil, quick-stop gel, styptic powder, or a bar of plain soap and apply it to the end of the bleeding nail. You can rub the soap across the end or stick the nail into the soap. You can purchase quick stop products at your pet supply store. With a rotary tool, the heat cauterizes. There is less risk of bleeding, but you can still cut too short.

If you don't notice the too-short nail right away and put your puppy down, you will see a trail of blood. It may look like a lot of bleeding, but it really isn't. Confine your puppy and apply treatment.

Special Considerations with a Rotary Tool

There are things to be aware of when using a rotary tool. Trim any fluffy hair on your pup's feet first or hold it back so it doesn't get caught in the tool. These tools heat up and can be painfully hot. Check to see how warm it feels.

Since there usually is no obvious blood, you can trim too far back—cauterizing but leaving the sensitive "quick" exposed. Be careful to trim just the hooks.

Dewclaws and Extra Toes

Most dogs have five toes on their front feet and four on the back. One of the toes in front is above the paw, along the leg. This is the "dewclaw" and may have been removed right after birth. In breeds such as Briards, Beaucerons, and Great Pyrenees, these extra toes are left on, and occur on the rear feet as well.

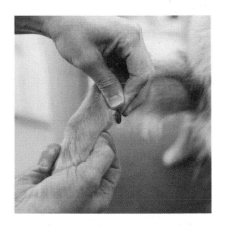

There is discussion about leaving dewclaws on. They must be trimmed, as they do not touch the ground and won't wear on their own. Without trims they can curl around and grow back into the pad. A loose dewclaw may get caught and pulled off. Dewclaws that are tight to the leg are safer.

Some researchers think dogs use their dewclaws when running or holding objects. Others feel the risk of injury is high enough to justify removal. Removal is generally done at 3 to 5 days of age. Your puppy may already have had his removed. Loose dewclaws may be removed when your pup is spayed or neutered.

Brushing

Your puppy will need brushing throughout her life. Even if you use a groomer, you will need to do some touchups at home between visits. Organize your equipment before you start: brushes, a comb, and a spray bottle with some plain water or dog hair conditioner. In the winter use an anti-static pet spray. Plan short sessions and use treats to make this a positive experience for your pup.

Short-Coated Puppies

Short-coated puppies really just need a good rubbing with a hound glove. This should loosen up any dead hair and remove it. You can follow this with a soft-bristle brush going in the direction of the hair coat. Be sure to moisten the coat lightly with the spray first. Breeds like Greyhounds and Weimaraners are truly wash and wear. You can probably get away with a weekly grooming.

Medium-Coated Puppies

Think of dogs like Labrador Retrievers as having a medium coat. Corgis and German Shepherd Dogs can fit into this category, too, though they also have a double coat with thick undercoat. This type of hair coat does not tend to mat, but these dogs do shed. The hound glove can help to loosen up dead hair, but you will have to follow that with a short pin brush, a slicker used gently, or a comb to actually remove the hair.

For the most part, brush in the direction the hair coat lies naturally. You may back-brush small areas during heavy shedding times. With this type of coat, if your puppy gets into mud, it is best to let him dry off first. Settle him in his crate with a nice chew. The dried mud should brush off easily.

Double-Coated and Long-Coated Dogs

Brushing gets a bit more complicated with the hairier dogs. Step one is to have your puppy lying on his side on a grooming table or on the floor with you next to him. Line brushing is the best way to make sure you groom all of his hair—not leaving clumps or mats in any areas.

Most puppies won't have the patience for a full grooming like this all at once. Try to do one area per session. Some puppies just love the grooming session and will even fall asleep! If your pup has trouble staying still, plan groomings after a walk or game has worn him out a bit.

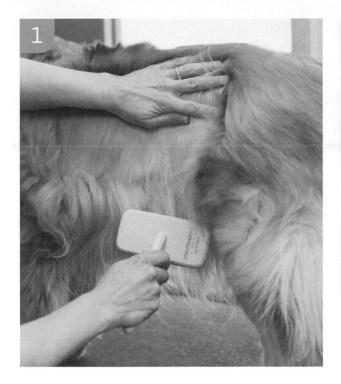

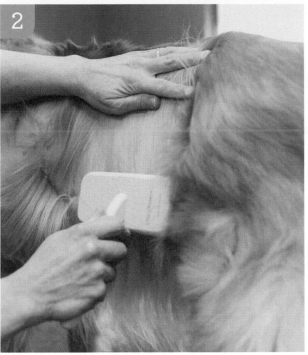

Start near the bottom—so way down on your puppy's side. Pick a small "line" of hair and brush upward first, then down.

Repeat this action, working your way up his side. You will need to do the same on both sides, his chest, and the top half of his legs.

Combs and Slickers

Combs and slicker brushes are used for feathers (the longer hair behind the front and rear legs) and on the tail if your puppy has a fluffy tail. The comb is also useful for removing hair when your pup is shedding.

Areas that tend to mat are the armpit and behind the ears. A comb can be used there to detangle hair. Be gentle—those are sensitive areas!

Removing Stuck-on Items

Puppies have a knack for getting into interesting things. Gum, pine pitch, and candy can get stuck in their coats. Handy solutions for loosening to remove them include oily lotions, peanut butter, and cooking oil. Of course, then you need to wash out those things!

Sometimes things are stuck on so tightly, your best solution is to cut them out. Have someone help to hold the pup. Keep your fingers or a comb between the pup's skin and your scissors as you cut. That will minimize the chances of accidentally nicking him.

Bathing

Bath time can be wild—especially the first couple of times for your puppy. Plan ahead, organizing your supplies so you don't leave the pup alone. Accept that you and the room you use will get wet. Keep your sense of humor. Visualize how lovely your puppy will look post-bath. Having a second person help is ideal.

Supplies to Organize

Have your shampoo and any conditioner you need by the tub or sink. Add a large towel—beach towels work well for any puppy above small-breed size. A waterproof slip lead is helpful. Have treats handy to reward your pup. Put cotton balls in your pup's ears to prevent water getting down in there. Some sterile ophthalmic ointment around the eyes to prevent soapy drips on the sensitive eye tissue is also a good idea.

Shampoos and Conditioners

There are many shampoos and conditioners. If your puppy came from a good breeder, she will have recommendations. Think about your pup's adult coat texture; that will guide you as well. Use medicated shampoos only if your pup has a skin problem.

Whether you need a conditioner may depend on the coat type. A silky coat may need conditioner to help prevent tangles and mats. Always check to see if conditioner or shampoo needs to be diluted before use.

Do not use human shampoo on your puppy. Human and dog skin have different pH levels. Human shampoos can also dry the skin. That said, a first bath with a baby or child's tearless shampoo is generally fine.

Setting Up the Tub or Sink

Place a nonslip mat on the bottom of the tub or sink. You don't want your pup to slip. If possible, switch your faucet head to a handheld sprayer so you can direct water where you need it to wet down the coat and rinse thoroughly.

Set the water at a tepid temperature before you add your puppy. Too hot will scald him. Too cold will chill him. Have your towel nearby to scoop him into when you are done.

The Bath

Wet your puppy thoroughly. Take a small amount of shampoo and dilute it in your hand or put it on your pup's coat and then add water. Lather him up fully, then rinse thoroughly. It is often easier to do all one side and then turn him to do the other side. If you don't rinse well, you may dry out the skin, causing dandruff and itching. Offer treats periodically.

Once your puppy is rinsed, he will want to shake. A good shake can shorten drying time as dogs are amazingly efficient at shaking off water. A gentle blow near his ear will usually result in a thorough shake. Then scoop him into the towel!

Drying

A short-coated puppy may dry with just a towel rub. Fluffy puppies will need a bit more help. You want your puppy dried completely so he won't get a chill. Human hair dryers get too hot for a puppy's delicate skin and hair. A blow dryer made for dogs will use tepid air to continue drying. If the puppy will only need occasional baths, you can also simply use multiple towels.

Some puppies are frightened by the sound and feel of a dryer. Turn the dryer on near but not touching him at first. Give treats so he learns the noise comes with good things. Start on the lowest setting. Never blow directly on his face or into his ears. Most puppies accept a dryer if you start by blowing on their backs or lower legs.

Some encounters—such as puppy and skunk—may call for an immediate bath. You can use a commercial skunk odor remover or make your own from this recipe: 1 quart hydrogen peroxide, ¼ cup baking soda, and 2 teaspoons liquid dish soap. Mix thoroughly—it will fizz a bit. Then soak your puppy with it, wait five minutes, and rinse thoroughly. Use this mix right away and don't store it.

Ears

Ear care will vary for your puppy depending on his ear type. Puppies with ears that prick or stand up tend to go through life with no problems. Ears that hang, especially if they are long and heavy, or are very hairy can be prone to problems. Make it a habit to examine your puppy's ears at least once a week.

Doing an Ear Check

Your puppy's ears should be a light pink when you look inside. With a hanging ear, you need to pick up the flap to look closely. There may be a very small amount of brown wax visible, but basically the ear should be clean and pink.

Routine Ear Care

Regular ear care is simple and easy. If your puppy has a clean, pink ear, do nothing! If there is a slight bit of brown discharge, wipe the ear gently with a cotton ball dampened with ear-cleaning solution. Do not use vinegar or alcohol—those would sting! Diluted vinegar may be used if your puppy swims a great deal and tends to get "swimmer's ear." But that is the only time to use it, and it should be under the guidance of your veterinarian.

When you do your weekly ear check, feel for mats behind the ears if your pup has little ear fringes. This is a common place for mats to develop. Trim them carefully—with a comb between the mat and the puppy's skin so the scissors do not cut him.

If the ear is red or inflamed or has a discharge, call your veterinarian. This is more than a grooming issue. Do not use cotton swabs in your pup's ear. The ear canal turns at the bottom, unlike a human ear, and you could damage tender tissues.

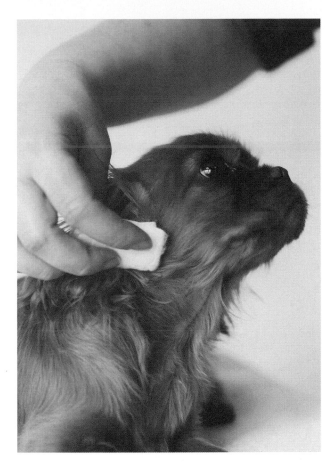

Signs of Problems

Potential problems in your pup's ears can be indicated by him scratching at his ears or rubbing his face and ears along the floor. Sometimes a puppy will whimper when doing this, or if you touch his ear or rub his head near the ears. This is a warning that there is a problem.

Looking down into the ear, a red, moist inflammation is not normal. That could mean a yeast infection—possibly related to water getting into the ear canal, or a food allergy. Dark brown discharge that looks like coffee grounds could be caused by ear mites. A bad smell, especially if accompanied by a pus-like discharge, means an ear infection. If your puppy shows any of these signs, you need to schedule a veterinary appointment.

If your pup is a prick-eared breed, like a German Shepherd Dog, but his ears aren't standing, don't despair. Some pups take a while to get their ears up. Teething may cause ears to droop. Do not give calcium supplements, as they won't help the ears—which are made of cartilage—but may damage your pup's joint development.

Eye Care

Your puppy's eyes may be the very reason you fell in love with him to begin with. You need to make sure those eyes stay clean and healthy. Eye care is usually simple and easy for a puppy.

Routine Care

Puppies do tend to stick their faces where they don't belong. That can mean dust, dirt, and lint blowing across their delicate eye tissues. It pays to wipe your pup's eyes gently every day, removing the corner "eye goobers." Use an approved eye wipe or a damp, warm washcloth.

If discharge has dried by the eye, you may need to compress the area first. Gently hold a damp, warm washcloth on the spot for a couple of minutes. Pet your pup and reassure him while you do this so he is not frightened. Most crusts soften up quickly and are easily removed.

Tear Stains

On some puppies, especially those with white fluffy faces, you will see a reddish-brown stain near the eyes. This is caused by the porphyrin pigment in tears that have overflowed the tear canal in the eye.

What causes extra tearing? Some puppies have small tear ducts that can't whisk away a large amount of tears. Others may have chronic irritation to the eyes, such as ingrown eyelashes. Living in a dusty area may cause irritation to the eyes. Some puppies tear a bit when they are teething. If your pup has fairly constant tear stains, have your veterinarian check for any medical cause such as an eyelash problem or a blocked tear duct.

You will read many remedies for eye stain removal for dogs. Some of these can be quite dangerous and damage sensitive eye tissues. Stick to cleaning the eyes with a diluted boric acid solution or artificial tears. Do this twice daily if needed. Using an antibiotic ointment may be effective for a while, but you risk building up antibiotic-resistant bacteria with long-term use.

Have your drinking water tested. High levels of minerals in the water may contribute to the staining. Keep facial hair trimmed away from the eyes. If your puppy has a medical reason for the excessive tearing, such as blocked tear ducts, have your veterinarian treat that by flushing the ducts.

Eye Discharges to Worry About

If your pup has a thick, goopy yellow or green discharge, you need to call your veterinarian. The thick discharge could be indicative of an infection in or around the eye itself. A bright yellow discharge in the spring or fall with no other signs may just be a pollen buildup. That should respond to flushing the eyes twice daily with artificial tears.

Most eye infections will be accompanied by pink swelling of the conjunctiva (tissues right around the eyeball) and/or squinting and holding the eye shut. If your pup shows any of these signs, contact your veterinarian right away. Eye problems can go from mild to bad very quickly.

Eye Injuries

Puppies with large, round eyes, like Pugs, are prone to eye injuries. In addition, they have short faces, so their eyes are right out in front and open to injury. Puppies also love to run through tall grass and weeds and roll on the ground, potentially picking up seeds and dirt in their eyes. They are low to the ground, so they are right down where sand blows and dust eddies occur.

Indoors puppies love to crawl under furniture and find dust bunnies. Also, forced-air heating can blow dust around at their eye level. You look into your puppy's eyes many times a day, but make a conscious effort to check them for any changes twice daily.

Anal Glands

Anal glands are at the less fun end of your puppy. These glands are located on either side of the puppy's rectum. Each time your puppy poops, these glands should empty a little bit. That discharge contributes to the "yuck" smell of fecal material. The anal gland discharge also tells other dogs that your puppy "was here." Think of it as leaving a calling card.

Routine Anal Gland Care

Some puppies and dogs go through life with no anal gland problems or need for attention. Others will occasionally get blocked up. Small-breed dogs tend to have more anal gland problems than bigger dogs.

Your regular care might involve helping to "express" the glands once a month.

1. Get another person to help.
2. The lucky person pets the puppy, steadies him, and feeds some treats.
3. The unlucky person gently lifts the tail straight up and, wearing a disposable glove, gently squeezes the sides of the rectum together while holding a paper towel over the area. Any discharge should be caught on the paper towel.

Anal Gland Problems

If you clean your puppy's glands and the discharge is not a thick yellow or gray color but looks bloody, your pup may have an infection. That calls for a visit to your veterinarian.

Most anal gland problems are noticed when a puppy drags his bottom on the floor or the ground. The dragging is due to a blocked gland that is not discharging a little bit with each bowel movement. As the gland fills up, the pressure is uncomfortable. This stimulates your pup to rub the area. You may also notice the puppy licking at this area.

Treating an Anal Gland Problem

If your puppy has an anal gland problem, your veterinarian will need to express the gland. If there are signs of infection, the puppy may need an antibiotic. Warm compresses over the area help ease discomfort. The compresses may also soften up the discharge so it empties more easily.

For recurrent anal gland problems, your veterinarian will give you a schedule for emptying the glands. She may also suggest adding some fiber to your pup's diet, which could be as simple as a teaspoon of plain canned pumpkin. The added fiber will put more pressure on the gland when your pup defecates and help it to empty.

Anal Gland Accidents

Anal glands are sometimes spontaneously emptied when a puppy gets frightened. Perhaps the smell is intended to scare off dangerous animals. When this happens, you will notice a very pungent, musky smell. You may find a brown-gray discharge sprayed around the area.

Reassure your pup and remember that this was an involuntary reaction. Wipe his rear carefully and then clean up the area that was sprayed. The plus is that you now know the glands are empty!

Finding a Groomer

You may decide that due to a lack of time or talent with clippers and scissors, grooming is best left to a professional. Your pup will need grooming for the rest of his life, so you want a groomer who will be the perfect fit for him.

Factors to Consider

You want a groomer who is convenient. If the groomer doesn't work on Saturdays and that is your only free day, it just won't work. Consider the distance to travel. If you have to drive 40 minutes each way, you may need to skip grooming appointments in bad weather. Make sure the groomer is comfortable with doing the type of trim you want your puppy to wear. Discuss fees. Find out if a nail trim is included or costs extra.

Most importantly, visit and get a feel for the groomer and her shop. Does she seem to genuinely enjoy the dogs? Is she patient with a wiggly pup? Are the dogs always supervised—during their bath, on the grooming table, and while behind a dryer in their crate? Of course there may be hair blowing all over, but is it generally a clean, well-cared-for shop?

Ask Around

One of the best ways to find a good groomer is to ask other people. Your veterinarian may have recommendations. The breeder, rescue, or shelter you got your puppy from may work with groomers they can recommend. Check with co-workers and fellow dog owners at your puppy class.

If neighbors have dogs, ask who they use. Pay special attention when you see someone with a dog groomed the way you envision your puppy looking. Don't hesitate to ask a stranger where they take their dog. Most people love to talk about their pets!

Local trade schools and grooming schools often offer discounted fees to attract clients for their students. Be aware that your puppy will most likely see a different person each time. These programs are very worthwhile but better for mature dogs.

The Mobile Option

Many communities now have mobile groomers. These groomers have vans with built-in bathing and drying equipment. They will schedule a time to arrive at your home and do your puppy's bath, trim, and blow dry right in your driveway. This can be a huge convenience for a busy family.

Do the same background research on a mobile groomer as on a groomer in a shop. Check out certifications and training. Ask for references.

Your Groomer's Background

Look for certification and membership in professional organizations. There are some excellent self-taught groomers, but most graduate from established schools or programs. Membership in a professional organization means the groomer keeps up to date on the latest tips for shampoos, trimming techniques, and equipment improvements.

Some of the established organizations include National Dog Groomers Association of America, International Professional Groomers, and the International Society of Canine Cosmetologists.

Be Clear About Your Expectations

Always try to be very clear with your groomer about what you expect. As you establish a relationship, this will go very easily, but at first it may be trial and error. Let the groomer know if you want your pup's feet trimmed or shaved close. Discuss how you picture your puppy's face looking post-trim: Will his eyes show or will he still need a barrette? Do you want a show-type clip or a pet-type clip?

Your groomer will also explain to you your responsibilities between grooming appointments. For example, you may need to comb your pup every other day to maintain his coat. If your puppy has any skin problems, your veterinarian may also be involved. She may dispense a medicated shampoo for you to have the groomer use.

Chapter 9

Health Care

- What to watch for
- Veterinarian visits and examinations
- Diseases, conditions, and emergency care

Every puppy comes with health care requirements. As with a human baby, you will face vaccination schedules, "well puppy" visits, and a host of preventive care initiatives. Preventive care tends to be much less expensive than treating problems after they happen.

Your new puppy should arrive with some health care information. In the packet from his breeder or the rescue or shelter group you should find basic health records. These should indicate vaccinations and dewormings, and preventive medication he has been given. This information is important because you don't want to duplicate treatments. Keep the originals of health records and make a copy for his veterinary clinic.

It's a good idea to have a binder for health care information, such as vaccination certificates and visit summaries. Any test results can also be kept there. You can track things like teething, height, weight, and behavior changes. Having all of his health information in one place could be important in case of an emergency. Include phone numbers such as Poison Control and the closest emergency veterinary clinic.

Your veterinary clinic will provide handouts on various health topics. The puppy's breeder may give you information—especially if his breed is noted for unusual problems. Copies of breed-specific health information can be given to your veterinarian.

Invest in a good-quality pet first aid book and a general canine health care book. Those reference books can help you decide if you need to make a middle-of-the-night or weekend trip to the emergency clinic.

Puppies require initial vaccinations and well-puppy checkups, and also are prone to injury from accidents. Veterinary costs will likely be high for the first year.

Signs of Trouble to Watch For

With a puppy things can go from fine to trouble very quickly. While most puppies fly through puppyhood unscathed, there can be problems that require veterinary attention.

Know the Normal

Knowing your puppy's "normals" is important. If your pup normally has three bowel movements a day, an alarm will go off when he has only two. If he usually has "midnight zoomies" but is lying quietly, you know to keep a close eye on him.

Normals refers to your pup's normal values. You can check his temperature occasionally, listen to his heart, or count his breaths to get actual number values. Most people develop a "feel" for their puppy's heart rate, respiratory rate, and temperature just from daily observation. If you notice anything unusual, pay close attention for the next 12 to 24 hours.

Observations to Concern You

If your puppy is panting heavily without reason—it's not a hot day, he hasn't been running—you should be concerned and watch him closely. Check his gum color. Most puppies have pink gums. You can press on the gum and it will blanch, but the color should return in a couple of seconds. This can be hard to do with a puppy with pigmented gums, however.

Any discharge from your pup's eyes or ears can be a cause for concern. A small amount of bright yellow matter in the corner of his eye during pollen season may just be pollen buildup. Watch for squinting or tearing. If he has a buildup of brown matter in his ears and acts like it hurts when you check or rub his ear, he may have an infection.

What Goes In and Comes Out

From housetraining your puppy you should have an idea what healthy stools look like. Loose stools or blood in the stool means a call to the veterinary clinic. Vomiting once is often not important, but if your puppy vomits more than once, and especially if he also has loose stools, make a visit to the clinic. Any blood in the vomit also means an immediate call to the clinic.

Straining to pass stool may mean constipation or an intestinal parasitic infection. Both are uncomfortable and deserve attention. The same is true for straining to pass urine. Urinary blockages are not common in puppies, but they are serious.

A loss of appetite is important in a puppy. This is especially true if he turns his nose up at more than one meal. The exception would be an abrupt change in diet. Puppies cannot afford to miss many meals—their size and metabolic rate require that they eat often.

A Limp

Puppies are known for twisting, slipping and sliding, or running into or off things. A yip followed by holding up a paw or limping for a few steps is generally not a serious concern. If your pup limps for more than five minutes, there may truly be an injury. Check for a broken toenail, but if the paw seems okay and he is still lame, his veterinarian should see him.

If your puppy has a crash, and totally holds a leg up and won't bear weight, there may be a significant injury. A pup with a fracture may nip when you examine the leg or pick him up. It is easier if you first wrap him gently in a towel.

Seizures

Any seizure should be considered an emergency. If your puppy is trembling or shivering badly, holding him may help. With a full-blown seizure, he will not be aware of who you are. Don't worry about him "swallowing his tongue"—this won't happen, and if you put your hand in his mouth you could be bitten. Scoop him up in a towel and have a family member or friend drive to the clinic while you hold him.

A depressed puppy could be post-seizure. If your puppy is acting quieter than normal, you need to watch him closely. Any collapse is a reason for concern.

Choosing a Veterinarian

Choosing a veterinarian is like choosing a pediatrician. You are choosing a doctor for someone who can't talk and who may not appreciate medical attention. You know early health care is important. You want someone who relates well to puppies, but who also is competent and up-to-date on the latest advances. Your veterinarian must be a good communicator, able to explain your pup's care to you.

Where to Start

Start with word-of-mouth referrals. Ask a neighbor or co-worker who has a dog where they go. The local shelter and rescue group may recommend a clinic. If your puppy's breeder lives nearby, she may give you a recommendation. Checking the phone book or an online listing of local clinics can be a help. You can rule out those that cater to cats only, and you might find some customer reviews.

Practical Considerations

Once you have some suggestions, you need to look at what your requirements are. If you work a typical 9-to-5 day and the clinic you are considering closes at 6 p.m. and has no weekend hours, that may not work for you. How close is the clinic to your home?

Look at emergency coverage. A clinic close by is wonderful, but if their emergency coverage is over two hours away, you may need to reconsider. With a single-veterinarian clinic you have to assume you will deal with other vets during an emergency. The same is true in group practices. You may have a favorite veterinarian, but you will likely need to see another veterinarian at times.

Practice Philosophy

An important thing to find out about a veterinary clinic is the practice philosophy. If preventive care and wellness are important to you, find a clinic that emphasizes those areas. Look for a clinic that stresses client/veterinarian partnerships.

Check the waiting area for handouts on pet care and responsible ownership. You want a veterinarian who looks at your puppy as a "total care" patient. Find out if referrals to specialists are offered or if there are specialists on staff.

A top veterinarian may not have the best bedside manners, but should be someone you feel comfortable with. You need to be comfortable asking questions, and receive answers you can understand.

Costs

While costs should not be the only consideration, the reality is you only have so much money for your puppy's health care. Does the clinic have arrangements for monthly payments if you have an emergency? Does the clinic accept or work with pet insurance companies? Most clinics will work out financial arrangements with regular clients they have developed a relationship with.

The Facility and Staff

While a veterinary clinic does not have to match a five-star hotel, it should be clean and in decent condition. Parking should be readily available. Ask about equipment such as radiography, ultrasound, and surgery suites. Some clinics do much of their blood work in house, while others send most of it out to associated laboratories. Both methods can work very well.

Look for staff who are friendly and upbeat as well as efficient. Do they seem genuinely interested in animals? Are they gentle with your puppy? A new puppy should have staff members oohing and aahing.

Emergency Clinics

Many communities have central veterinary emergency clinics. Find the closest one to you, and see if your veterinarian sends after-hours referrals there. Do the same "word-of-mouth" check of the emergency clinic. See if they have the latest equipment to deal with emergencies, including both surgeries and medical support.

Preparing Your Puppy for the Vet Visit

There are some simple preparations for your puppy's veterinary visits that can make things go smoothly for both of you. Do these ahead of time and the visit will be pleasant, plus you'll make much more effective use of your time in the office with the veterinarian and veterinary technician.

Paperwork

Be sure to bring any relevant paperwork. Copies of your puppy's health record will save your pup from unnecessary vaccinations or treatments, and save your pocketbook from unnecessary fees. It also helps the clinic staff plan what care your pup will need in the future.

Along with the puppy's health record, bring copies of any health screenings done on his parents. Information on any DNA testing of his parents will be important to the clinic.

If your puppy is from a local shelter or rescue group, you may have a coupon or certificate for a free exam. Be sure to bring that along with you! If you found coupons or discounts online for medications such as heartworm preventives or flea control products, bring those as well. Most veterinary clinics will honor them.

The Trip

Hopefully you have taken your puppy on some short drives to fun places. Many clinics will also let you drop by for weekly weigh-ins at no charge. On those visits, make sure your pup gets some loving and a few good treats. You want the veterinary visit to be a positive experience.

Ideally your pup should travel in a secured crate. A canine seat belt is the next best option. He should not ride loose or in your lap, especially if you are driving. It helps if you have a family member or friend along to help with the puppy while you sign in and deal with clinic forms.

Your List

The week before your visit, start a list of questions. By writing them down, you won't forget in the excitement of dealing with the puppy and the office visit. Put down any and all concerns—how much to feed, what preventive medications you need for heartworm or tick control, etc.

Be honest about any problems you are having. If your pup cries much of the night, doesn't eat well, or seems to need to urinate every hour, your veterinarian can offer some help. If you have not written these things down ahead of time, you tend to forget while everyone is admiring your cute canine. Have some extra paper to write down responses.

Know what food you are feeding and how much you are giving. The "bag with the cute dog on the front" could be any number of products and "a handful" can vary between you and your spouse. The more accurate information you can provide your veterinarian, the more effective she will be in developing a health plan for your puppy.

Fecal Sample

It is important to bring a fecal or stool sample from your pup. A tablespoon-size amount is plenty—put this in a resealable plastic bag. Due to the life cycle of many internal parasites, sometimes multiple dewormings are required to kill all of the parasites. The veterinary technician will examine the sample for any parasites or parasite eggs.

MDR 1 is a DNA test done at Washington State University to look for a genetic mutation involving the metabolism of certain drugs. Knowing your puppy's status (from testing his parents or him) could help guide your veterinarian to find safe drug choices in an emergency. This is most important for herding breed puppies and herding breed mixes.

The Physical Examination

The physical examination is the most important part of your puppy's visit. Your veterinarian will check him from nose to tail tip and all the parts in between. A thorough exam will pick up any underlying problems your pup might have. Your veterinarian will then discuss options for treatment and care. Plan on monthly exams for your puppy until 4 to 6 months of age, then schedule an exam at 1 year.

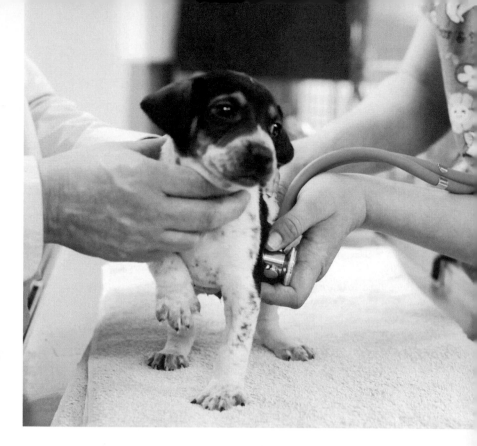

Head First

Your veterinarian will start at your pup's head. She will look in his eyes, check his ears, and examine his mouth. She or a technician will check any discharge from the ears on a microscope slide.

While looking in the mouth, your vet is checking your pup's bite (his *occlusion,* or how his teeth come together) and how his teething is progressing. Gums will be checked for good color and quick refill after pressure.

The Chest and Forelimbs

Next, the veterinarian will listen to your pup's heart and lungs with a stethoscope. Some puppies have "innocent" murmurs that will disappear over time. Other murmurs could indicate problems. Lung sounds should be soft and not raspy.

It is important to also *palpate,* or manually examine, the chest, feeling for any discrepancies in the anatomy and checking weight and muscles. Your veterinarian will also run her hands down your puppy's front legs, and compare the legs for conformation and condition. If your pup has a difference in musculature between the legs, the vet will look for the cause.

Abdomen

Puppies are notorious for round bellies, but that is not always a good sign. Your veterinarian will palpate for normal structures and check for excess gas or weight. Parasites can also cause a rounded abdomen; they would be detected on the fecal sample you brought.

Your puppy should not feel pain or fuss during an abdominal palpation. Any hernias, either umbilical or in the groin area, would be noted at this time. Small umbilical hernias may close up on their own, while others require surgery. Hernia repairs are often done at the same time as spaying or neutering.

Back and Hind Limbs

Running a hand along your pup's back is one way a veterinarian can detect problems with alignment and any asymmetries. Muscle mass should be equal on both sides of the spine. The spine should run straight back into the pelvis and tail.

Your veterinarian will run her hands down both rear legs, doing a comparison just like for the front legs. Any pain or swelling will mean a closer look. The tail will be checked for kinks or other abnormalities.

Overall Impressions

While looking at individual parts of your puppy, the veterinarian is also making some general assessments. She is looking at your pup's muscle and body condition. Is your pup a bit too chubby, or maybe a tad underweight?

What is the condition of the hair coat? Puppy hair can be slightly dull and fuzzy, but bright, shiny hair should be coming in. Are any fleas or ticks noted? What about parasites like tapeworms that leave dry rice-like segments near the tail? Is there dried fecal matter under the tail, hinting at loose stools?

What is your pup's mental attitude? Is he outgoing and friendly, or a bit reserved? Is he showing any signs of anxiety, or is he a bit too pushy or aggressive? Your veterinarian will note all of these things and make recommendations to improve anything that is not normal.

History and Background

Your vet will also ask you questions as she examines your puppy. Where did the pup come from? Did you meet the parents? If so, what were they like? What is he eating? How are his stools? Are you having any problems with housetraining?

At this time, your list of questions and observations can be invaluable. Between you and the veterinarian, any possible problems or concerns should be identified.

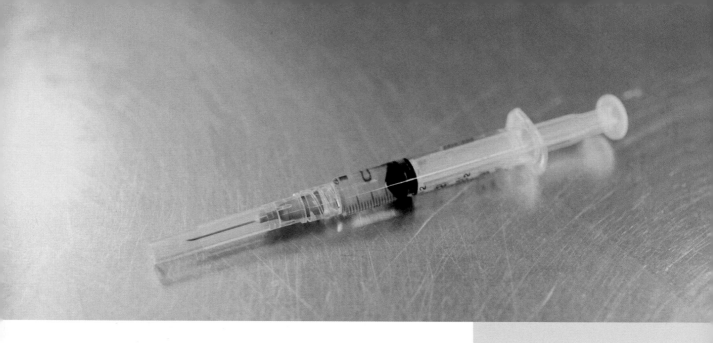

Vaccinations

The topic of vaccinations has become a hot button for many veterinarians and pet owners. Be prepared to do some research and make a custom plan for your puppy. Not all dogs need all vaccines. The timing for boosters is now being looked at with serious research as well.

Core Vaccines

Core vaccines are defined as vaccines every dog should have. The core vaccines cover diseases that are serious and often fatal. These diseases tend to be found everywhere, so you can almost count on your puppy being exposed at some point. The basic core vaccines are

- Rabies
- Distemper
- Parvo
- Canine adenovirus

These are all viral diseases. In addition to being important for your pup's health, the rabies vaccine is required by law and is important for human health considerations as well.

A titer can be done at 16 weeks to verify your puppy's immune status. A titer looks at a blood sample and checks whether your pup has developed immunity to a specific disease-causing agent. Titers can be done throughout your puppy's life to verify the need for boosters. The one possible exception is rabies; some state laws require booster vaccinations and will not accept titers.

When to Start Vaccinations

Your pup's initial vaccinations are timed to minimize any risk periods—when your pup would be without useful immunity. This is truly a balancing act. Your puppy got some immunity from his mother. That maternal immunity wears off somewhere between 6 and 16 weeks in most puppies. While the maternal immunity is high, your pup's own immune system won't kick in.

The catch is timing things so your puppy can start developing his own immunity right about the same time as the maternal immunity wears off. This is why puppies get an initial series of vaccines. Current recommendations suggest starting at 8 or 10 weeks with the first dose. Give a booster one or two times at monthly intervals until the pup is 14 to 16 weeks of age. By 16 weeks you can feel fairly confident that the puppy has some of his own immunity.

Boostering

After the initial series of vaccinations, most veterinarians recommend a booster one year later and then every three years. Research is ongoing to verify a long-lasting immunity from most of the viral vaccines. That could mean stretching boosters out to every five or seven years, or possibly not requiring them at all. The use of titers can be substituted for boosters in many cases if there are concerns about immune status.

Bacterial vaccines, called *bacterins*, are not so long lived. Many of these vaccines stimulate short-term immunity—possibly as short as six months to one year. Depending on your pup's individual risk, you may need to do additional boosters for these problems.

Non-Core Vaccines

The non-core vaccines are felt to be optional for at least some dogs. Leptospirosis and Borrelia (for Lyme disease) are two of these vaccines. If your pup has minimal risk of exposure, he may never need these two bacterins. On the other hand, if the puppy is likely to be exposed to ticks carrying Lyme disease or to an environment where Leptospirosis is known to exist, your veterinarian may recommend these vaccines.

The vaccines for most of the canine cough syndrome culprits may be required at a boarding kennel you want to use on occasion. There are a number of vaccines associated with canine cough syndromes. Your veterinarian can guide you as to which of those vaccines makes sense for your puppy if you have to board him.

There are some non-core vaccines that can almost always be avoided. The giardia vaccine is for a protozoal illness that is generally mild and relatively easy and inexpensive to treat. Very few puppies would need this vaccine. The vaccine for a rattlesnake bite can be skipped if you don't live in rattlesnake country. The vaccine for canine oral melanoma is only given to dogs who suffer from this cancer.

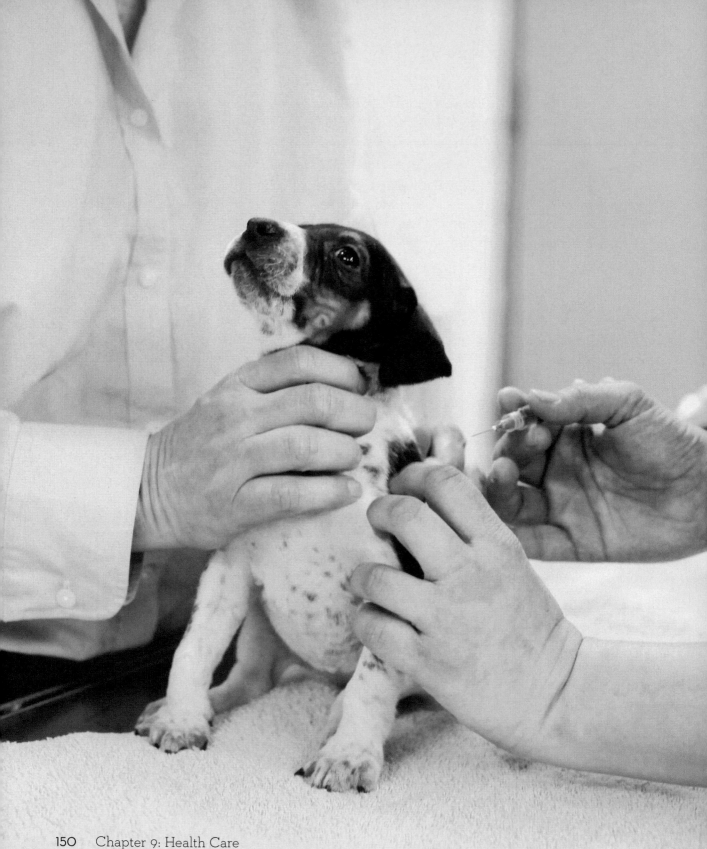

After the Vaccination

Many, but not all, puppies will be a bit tired and possibly cranky for about 24 hours after a vaccination. Your pup may also be a touch sore at the site of the vaccination. Generally just letting your pup "wear it off" works best. If your pup does not perk up in a day, vomits, has diarrhea, or develops swelling at the vaccination site or around his muzzle with associated trouble breathing, you need to contact your veterinarian.

Serious vaccine reactions are not common, but anaphylactic shock is a rare occurrence. Swelling of the face and in the neck area generally occur within a short time of vaccination, accompanied by difficulty breathing. Some veterinary clinics have you wait around for about 30 minutes after your pup's vaccination to watch for any reaction. Any puppy who has had a vaccine reaction should rely on titers as much as possible in the future.

Spaying and Neutering

Spaying and neutering are surgeries that remove the reproductive capabilities of your puppy. A pup who has been spayed or neutered will not produce puppies. Traditionally puppies had this surgery done at about 6 months of age, but research has indicated some other options might be better.

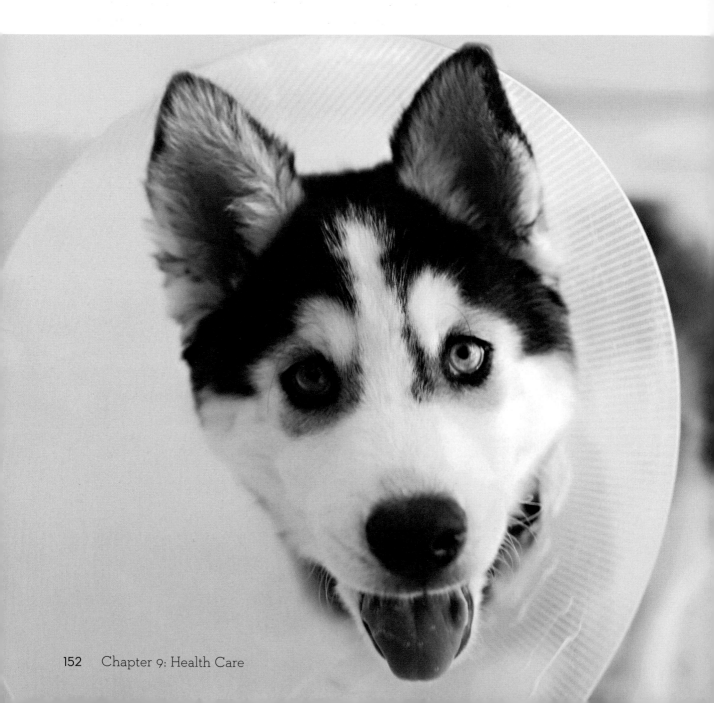

Timing

Many shelters and rescues like to have puppies spayed or neutered before they go off to their new homes. This led to a trend of performing these surgeries on puppies as young as 8 to 12 weeks of age. The plan was to guarantee that the puppies would not grow up, reproduce, and add to the pet overpopulation problem. Your puppy may have already had this surgery done if he came from a shelter or a rescue. These really early spay/neuters are now starting to fall out of favor.

Six months of age has been touted as the best time for surgery. This timing generally catches female dogs before their first heat and reduces the chances of developing breast cancer by 90 percent. That percentage drops with each heat a puppy goes through.

Pluses of Spaying and Neutering

A traditional spay removes both the uterus and ovaries, so it also removes any chance of your puppy developing uterine cancer or uterine infections.

Traditional neutering means removing both testicles from a male puppy. Neutering can reduce the chances of certain types of hernias and perianal cancers as well as prostate enlargement that comes with age. Some undesirable male behaviors such as urine marking tend to decrease in neutered males.

Minuses of Spaying and Neutering

Some recent research has suggested that even waiting until 6 months may not be in the best interest of your puppy. Spaying and neutering before the growth plates have closed can lead to an adult dog with weaker joints. Early spayed or neutered dogs tend to be taller and spindlier than littermates left intact. Underdeveloped bones and muscles may predispose active and sporting dogs to injury. Waiting until 12 to 18 months may be a better choice for many dogs.

Two studies looked at the development of cancer in relation to spayed/neutered status. The studies looked at Golden Retrievers and Rottweilers, both breeds that have a predisposition to certain types of cancers. The studies showed an increase in certain cancers in the dogs who had surgery. Much more research needs to be done in this area to see if this is a valid conclusion and can be applied to other breeds, but it certainly gives pause for thought.

A puppy with a retained testicle (or two) will need to have the internal testicle removed. Some owners choose to have their male neutered at that time, while others may choose to only have the retained testicle removed. This surgery is closer to a spay surgery, with an abdominal incision to find the testicle that did not drop into the scrotum. While ideally both testicles are in the scrotum by 8 to 10 weeks of age, most veterinarians would recommend waiting six months or more before surgery. Retained testicles do have an increased risk for cancer, but that does not usually happen until well into canine middle age.

Some New Alternatives

Some variations on the traditional spay and neuter surgeries are now offered. Some veterinarians will simply remove the ovaries from a female dog, leaving the uterus as a more natural state. This will provide some of the hormones an intact female would have. With the ovaries gone, the risk of an infected uterus is greatly reduced.

For male puppies, there is now an injectable medication that makes them sterile while preserving most of the male hormones such as testosterone. This has been used in Europe and is now approved for use in the United States. There are also veterinarians who are comfortable with doing vasectomies on male dogs. Again, this makes them sterile while preserving many of the hormones.

Living with an Intact Dog

If you decide to leave your female puppy intact, you will deal with her "heat periods" from one to three times a year. Most dogs show heats twice a year, but it does vary with the breed. During those three weeks you will need to keep your puppy away from any possible male suitors. Special panties can be worn to help with the discharge—which is bloody at times. Your pup should only go out on lead, even in your fenced yard, and always accompanied by an adult. Giving chlorophyll pills can help to reduce the attractive odors an intact female gives off, but it won't totally mask them. Dogs in heat are banned from some competitions, training classes, and day care facilities.

An intact male dog may show a tendency to urine mark, including in the house. If there is a female in heat in the neighborhood, your male pup may whine, fuss, and pace. Some males may run off, even traveling a mile or more, to find the girl of their dreams. Intact males may also have more problems getting along with other dogs.

Your responsibility as an owner increases if you choose to have intact dogs. Most families aren't truly prepared to have a litter of puppies. If you follow reputable practices, you need to do health screenings on both parents. You should have your dog's conformation and temperament evaluated by an objective mentor.

Raising puppies means a huge commitment of time and money. You need to provide all of the early socialization experiences and stay on top of early health care. Reputable breeders also stay involved with the puppies they produce for life. They are always willing to take back any puppy—even 10 or 12 years down the line. That is a huge responsibility!

Not all dogs need to or should be bred. Even if you choose to keep your pup intact, you can enjoy him or her as a companion without getting into the expense and hassle of breeding.

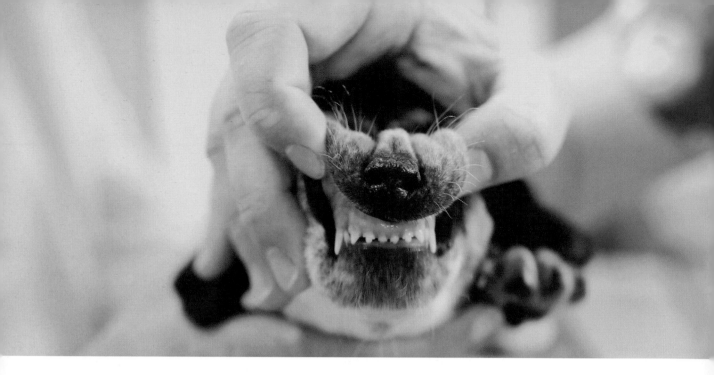

Teeth

Your puppy's teeth and mouth are very important—not only for eating but also for carrying things. Good dental health and habits start out in puppyhood. Proceed slowly and establish a good dental routine.

How Many Teeth and When?

Four weeks: Your pup started teething at about 4 weeks of age. The first teeth are "baby" or deciduous teeth. These are sharp little teeth, and the canine teeth have a tight curve in them. These are the puppy teeth that tend to get caught on things—including your hands if you aren't careful!

Four to six weeks: From 4 to about 6 weeks of age your puppy gets more teeth. The normal full set of deciduous teeth is 28 total. Some breeds, such as the hairless breeds, will naturally have fewer.

Three to eight months: From 3 to 8 months of age, your pup will gradually lose his baby teeth as adult teeth grow in. Adult teeth are sturdier and less sharp, and have deeper roots. In addition, there are more of them—a normal adult dog has 42 teeth.

Many families try to find and save baby teeth. You may notice blood on a toy and see the empty spot. Bleeding is minimal. Some baby teeth break off while the pup is chewing a hard object. The root will dissolve on its own. You may find a couple, but many simply disappear—lost in a carpet or chew toy or swallowed by your pup.

What About Retained Teeth?

Normally, as the adult teeth push up through the gums, the baby teeth will fall out. Occasionally a puppy will retain a baby tooth for a bit. This is most common with the canine teeth. If your pup has "double fangs," don't panic. The baby tooth will almost always fall out as the root resorbs by itself.

Sometimes a baby tooth refuses to leave. Its presence can cause the adult tooth to grow in at an angle. Sometimes the adult tooth will become impacted and can't get through the gum at all. In those cases, the baby tooth will need to be removed by your veterinarian.

Teething Problems

Just like human babies, some puppies have a rough time when teething. Their gums are sore, they may run a low fever, and they don't want you touching their mouths. If you need to check your pup's mouth, do so very gently and follow up with a soft treat.

There are ways to help your puppy at this time. A damp washcloth left in the freezer provides a cold but fairly soft chew item. Do this only under supervision, as you don't want your pup chewing and eating the cloth! There are commercial products made for teething relief, and some are refrigerated for additional soothing. Raw carrots are another favorite puppy chew item during teething.

Starting Dental Care

Avoid handling your pup's mouth during painful teething times, but you can still get him started on a good dental routine. Daily brushing is the gold standard for dog dental care.

Start with a soft children's toothbrush, a pet toothbrush, or a finger brush of soft rubber. A piece of gauze will work as well. Choose a flavored pet toothpaste. Most puppies prefer chicken or tuna flavors, though some like malt or mint. Avoid human products, as human toothpaste is not meant to be swallowed.

At first, simply let your pup lick the toothpaste off and chew on the brush a bit. Gradually move to sliding the brush along the gum line under the lip. Don't make a big production out of opening the mouth. You can do plenty of good just sliding under the lips. Try to do this daily.

Internal Parasites

Internal parasites are an area of concern for all dogs, but especially for puppies. Puppies don't have a lot of extra body condition to cover lost nutrients. That is especially true of toy and small-breed puppies.

Many internal parasites can infect people as well as dogs. Some parasite eggs and larvae can survive for long periods in the environment and cause reinfections. Many adult dogs have built up some natural immunity to internal parasites, but puppies have not. A parasite infection can easily grow and overwhelm a young pup.

Roundworms

Roundworms or ascarids are a very common parasite found in puppies. These parasites can stay encysted in a female dog and only activate if she is bred and has puppies. The puppies can even be infected in utero. This is a parasite with serious potential human complications.

In puppies, roundworms migrate through the liver and lungs, causing some scarring, but most of the damage is due to stealing nutrients in the intestines. Puppies with heavy worm loads don't gain weight well, have poor hair coats, and show big potbellies. Adult worms may eventually be passed in the stool or vomited up. These are large worms that look like spaghetti.

The CAPC recommends deworming puppies every two weeks from 2 until 8 weeks of age, or whenever they go on a monthly heartworm preventive that covers roundworms as well. Roundworms can be diagnosed by finding an adult worm or, more commonly, through a fecal exam by your veterinarian. Luckily, many dogs develop some natural immunity against roundworms as they age.

Hookworms

Hookworms are another intestinal parasite that is commonly found in puppies. This parasite can infect puppies via nursing from a mother who is infested. Hookworms are smaller than roundworms and the adults are rarely seen.

These worms drain nutrients like the roundworms, but really concentrate on blood and can actually make a puppy anemic. Bloody diarrhea, dehydration, and even death can occur with a heavy infestation. Larvae can get into the skin of both dogs and humans if they walk over contaminated ground, causing skin infections as they migrate in.

Early and regular deworming is important here. Be sure to have your puppy's fecal sample checked on his well-puppy visits.

Tapeworms

Tapeworms are a secondary parasite that can be seen in your puppy. Families may notice what look like dried rice in the hair around their puppy's rectum or small, squiggly worms in the stool. Those are tapeworm segments.

Puppies can get tapeworms one of two ways. The most common is from fleas. If your puppy chews on his flea bites and accidentally eats a flea, he may be ingesting early-stage tapeworms as well. The second way is by eating rodents that are intermediate hosts.

Tapeworms are easy to treat, but unless you get rid of fleas or stop the hunting, they will come back.

Children playing on contaminated ground can accidentally ingest ascarid eggs and larvae. The larvae then migrate throughout the child's body causing serious damage, including to the liver or the eyes. The Companion Animal Parasite Council (capcvet.org) has guidelines for treating parasites in pets.

Whipworms

Whipworms are a fairly small but potentially deadly intestinal parasite in puppies and dogs. These parasites tend to cause bloody diarrhea, weight loss, and anemia. A heavy load may cause death. Puppies need to ingest eggs from the environment to become infected. Dogs do not seem to build up any natural immunity to whipworms.

Whipworms can be difficult to diagnose. A fecal sample is the ideal way, by finding eggs under the microscope. Unfortunately, whipworms don't shed eggs as often as some of the other intestinal parasites. If your veterinarian suspects a whipworm infestation, she may prescribe deworming even with a negative fecal sample. Better to be safe than sorry in this case!

Coccidia

Coccidia are another intestinal parasite that is most commonly seen in puppies. These protozoal parasites can cause weight loss and dehydration due to nutrient drain. Your puppy can get coccidia from eating oocysts (protozoal eggs) in the environment, or rarely from eating an intermediate host such as a mouse.

The infective stage is quite hardy and can survive in the environment—even in a kennel area. Strong disinfectants are required to clean an area that has been infected. Coccidia require different medications for treatment than the standard dewormers. Sulfa drugs top the list of effective treatments.

Diagnosing coccidia infection is also done via fecal sample, but the sample is handled differently than for the nematode parasite problems like roundworms and hookworms. If your veterinarian suspects a coccidial infection, she will evaluate the sample for both types of parasites.

Giardia

Giardia are protozoal organisms that can infect dogs. They damage the intestinal lining of an infected dog. This causes problems with both digestion and absorption of nutrients, leading to a malnourished puppy. An infected pup may have diarrhea, vomiting, and abdominal pain.

Like whipworms, giardia can be tricky to diagnose, as the immature stages are not shed all the time. A fecal sample needs to be evaluated in a couple of ways to find this parasite—including a special giardia-specific diagnostic test.

Giardia cysts can exist both on contaminated ground and in water sources. You may hear the term "beaver fever" associated with giardia. Many wildlife species can pass giardia cysts into water sources. For this reason, you should carry drinking water for both you and your puppy while hiking. Do not let your pup drink from unknown creeks and ponds.

While there is no officially approved medication to treat giardia, a number of dewormers have been shown to be effective and safe for use in infected puppies.

Stress, Contamination, and Intestinal Parasites

Intestinal parasites have the greatest success in puppies that are stressed. That might be mental stress from moving to their new homes or physical stresses, such as being cold or hungry. Doing your part to provide your puppy good food, a warm, safe place to stay and sleep, and plenty of social company can help him fight off these parasites.

Contaminated ground and water sources can hinder your fight to keep your pup free of these parasites. Avoid walking your puppy in areas where many dogs, especially stray dogs, may eliminate. Always pick up after your puppy so you don't contribute to contamination if your pup is shedding eggs. Don't let your puppy drink standing water on your hikes; you should even bring your own water and bowl to places like a dog park.

Heartworms

Heartworms are a slightly different class of internal parasites. These worms live in the heart and lungs of infected dogs—not the intestines. The immature stages, called microfilaria, are found in the bloodstream. Heartworm can be fatal by causing permanent damage to both the heart and lungs.

Heartworms are spread by mosquito bites. A mosquito bites a dog infected with heartworm and then spreads it to another dog in its next meal. Originally heartworm only occurred in "pockets" around the United States, but it has now been diagnosed in dogs throughout the country.

Heartworm is diagnosed by a variety of blood tests. Some look for antibodies and antigens while others look for microfilaria in the sample. Treating heartworm is long, complicated, and expensive. As the parasites die, they need to dissolve inside the dog's body. This can lead to deadly emboli in the lungs. This is definitely a disease to prevent rather than to treat!

Prevention is generally started by a blood test to verify that your dog is not currently infected with heartworm. Young puppies who have not been exposed to a mosquito season may be exempted. Your veterinarian will discuss that with you.

Most families choose to use the once-a-month preventives for their puppies. Most of these come in a chewable form that puppies happily eat as a treat. The preventives also provide protection or treatment for most of the intestinal parasites, including hookworms and roundworms.

Be prepared to treat all your dogs if your puppy turns out to be shedding parasite eggs. While adult dogs often have some natural immunity, you don't want them recycling the parasites back to your puppy.

External Parasites

External parasites can be the bane of a dog owner's existence. Many of the parasites are happy snacking on humans as well as puppies. In addition to the itching and discomfort, they may carry deadly diseases. It is easier to prevent these pests than to treat and remove after they have moved in to your puppy's life and your home. It is important to realize that external parasites can be found almost everywhere. While fleas can't survive at high altitudes, many types of mites can. Ticks tend to live in heavy concentrations in certain areas but they can be found from cities to farms.

Mites

These tiny parasites can live in the skin, like demodectic or sarcoptic mites, or on the surface. They may cause itching and hair loss. The term "mange" is associated with mites. They can cause secondary infections from the damage they do to the puppy's skin. Luckily, they do not tend to cause serious diseases.

Demodectic Mites

Demodex or red mange is caused by a mite that lives burrowed into the skin of a dog or puppy. Most of the time, the dog and these mites coexist without problems. However, many puppies have mild cases of demodex as their immune system gets organized.

The mild cases of demodex start with some hair loss, often around the head, on the muzzle, or around the eyes. Occasionally, there will be circles of hair loss on the legs. These areas are generally seen on puppies younger than 6 months. Most puppies will "outgrow" cases of localized demodex. Your veterinarian will diagnose this by doing a simple skin scrape in a hairless area. The cigar-shaped mites are evident under a microscope.

The problem comes when a puppy's immune system is overwhelmed for whatever reason and the mites reproduce out of control. The puppy will have large areas with hair loss and associated skin infections. Now you have an itchy puppy with areas of red, oozing skin. Diagnosis is via a skin scrape. Your puppy will need a shave if he is longhaired and then a series of Amitraz dips to kill the mites. In addition, he may need antibiotics, medicated shampoos, and immune stimulants to help him conquer these invaders. Spaying is recommended for female puppies as the heat cycles seem to intensify the mites and lead to relapses.

Sarcoptic Mites

Sarcoptic mites cause a very itchy mange. Puppies with these mites will itch and itch. They are also diagnosed by a skin scrape. Even if no mites are found, your veterinarian will start treatment if she suspects sarcoptic mange. Sarcoptic mange mites will spread to people. The mites can come from wildlife, such as squirrels, and may spread from dog to dog. Secondary skin infections are common, as a puppy may scratch so hard it causes skin sores. There are collars and topical medications that control or cure sarcoptic mange. Medicated baths and antibiotics are often necessary due to skin infections.

Fleas

Fleas are external parasites that reproduce quickly. They feed on almost any living being—including your puppy and you! Fleas are found almost everywhere, city or country, except areas of high altitude and low humidity. They infest a number of species, including wildlife.

If you notice your puppy scratching, pull back his hair (especially around the tail area) and look for running brown blurs. Those are fleas. You might also notice what looks like salt and pepper grit in that area. Take a pinch and put it on a piece of white tissue and add a drop of water. If it turns red, that was flea poop.

Another way to spot fleas is to quickly roll your puppy over. Any fleas that are exposed to the light will run across the lightly haired groin area and be easily seen. If you find one flea, assume there are others and that all of your pets and your house are infested.

Always read the directions on any flea medications carefully. Only use products approved for puppies. Do not use dog medications on your cat if you have one. Call your veterinarian right away if you see drooling, vomiting, or a wobbly gait.

Flea-Related Problems

A heavy load of fleas could cause anemia in your puppy. Some dogs also develop a severe allergic reaction that requires medical attention in addition to flea removal. If you get fleabites, you might itch a bit or develop an allergic reaction yourself. Fleas are capable of carrying some other problems into your puppy's life. Tapeworms, an internal parasite, are one possibility. In addition, some serious illnesses could spread to your puppy or you via fleas, including plague and typhus (although these are very rare).

Treating Fleas

Think of fighting fleas as running a battle campaign. You need to take direct and complete action. You must treat your pets—all of them, not just your puppy—and your house. Treating outside areas is important, too.

A quick flea shampoo is a good start. Follow that with a topical flea preventive medication approved for puppies. You may choose to treat the house yourself (especially if it is a mild infestation) or hire an exterminator. Ask about options for outdoors, such as spreading a powder called diatomaceous earth or using a pet-safe spray.

As with so many health problems, it is better to prevent a flea problem. Ask your veterinarian about a suitable topical preventive to use on your puppy. Be sure to adjust the dose as he grows.

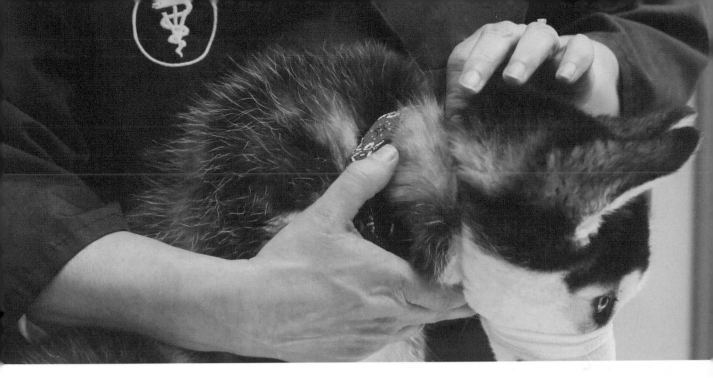

Ticks

Ticks are not as athletic as fleas but are even more feared. Ticks tend to attach to a puppy in small numbers, but they can spread deadly diseases.

Your puppy can pick up ticks any time of year, though they are most common in the spring and fall. Generally ticks are picked up as your puppy walks through tall grass or underbrush where ticks live. They let go of the plants and attach to your pup.

A heavy infestation of ticks could lead to anemia, but other problems are more common. Ticks can spread a variety of serious illnesses, including many that can also affect people. These diseases include Lyme Disease, Rocky Mountain Spotted Fever, and ehrlichia.

Finding Ticks

Check your puppy after every walk through areas with tall grass or brush. Run your hands over him carefully feeling for any bumps. Ticks often attach around the head and ears or the front legs. Once a tick has attached, it will expand due to the blood it sucks. Use gloves or special tick-removal tools to take ticks off your puppy.

Treating for Ticks

The first step is to remove any ticks you find. Your veterinarian may recommend a follow-up blood test to check for any tick-related diseases. Then apply a topical medication that repels ticks. Some special medicated collars will also help in flea and tick control.

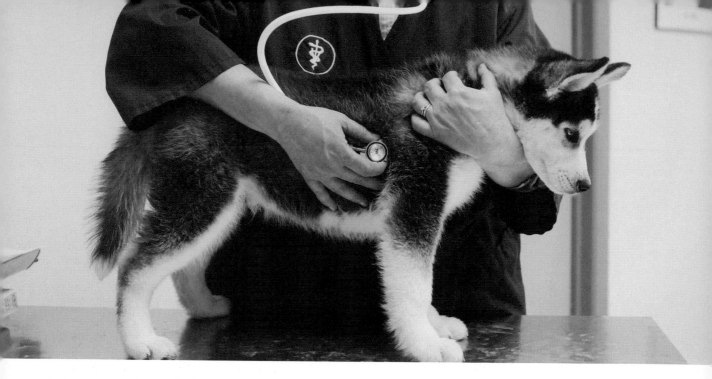

Heart Problems

Heart problems can show up in young puppies, and are different problems than you would find in older dogs. Most commonly these are congenital—meaning a defect found at birth of unknown cause—or a genetic defect. Some heart problems are minor, but others can be life-threatening. Your veterinarian will listen to your pup's heart on each well-puppy visit.

There are heart defects that are more commonly seen in particular breeds, but puppies of any breed or mix can be born with a heart problem. Puppies with heart defects tend to lag behind their normal littermates in growth and activity. Puppies with severe defects will die without treatment—generally within a year.

Murmurs

Some puppies will show a slight murmur in their first veterinary exam. A murmur means there is some turbulence in the blood flow through the heart that your veterinarian can hear with her stethoscope. Most of these are "innocent" murmurs—which your puppy will outgrow. Always follow up a report of a murmur to verify that it goes away.

Some murmurs indicate a defect in the anatomy of the heart. These are often fairly loud, are localized to one area of your pup's heart, and may require surgery or medical care and lifestyle adjustments. If your veterinarian detects a murmur that indicates a problem, she will suggest a cardiac ultrasound or other tests to help identify the problem exactly.

PDA or Patent Ductus Arteriosus

When in utero, your puppy's blood flow bypasses his lungs, as they are not functioning yet. After birth, the bypass, called the ductus arteriosus, should close. If it remains open, your puppy will not receive enough oxygenated blood for normal growth.

The murmur from a PDA is quite loud and easily heard via a stethoscope. It can sometimes be felt when you gently hold your puppy's chest. Surgery is necessary to repair this defect, closing off the open channel so all blood is rerouted through the lungs. Most puppies come through surgery fine and then have normal life spans.

Stenosis Defects

Stenosis defects occur when major blood vessels around the heart are narrower than normal. The heart has to work much harder to pump blood through these smaller vessels. If the pulmonary artery is involved, this is called pulmonic stenosis. Minor cases may not need treatment, but severe ones respond to surgery.

When the opening to the aorta is narrow, this is called SAS, or subaortic stenosis. Puppies suffering from SAS may collapse and are very quiet and lethargic due to a lack of oxygen. These puppies require surgery.

Valve Defects

Valve defects involve the valves of the heart that open and close as the heart pumps blood from one chamber to the next. A defective valve allows blood to "leak" backwards. This increases the workload on that chamber of the heart. Holes in the walls (septa) of the heart's chambers have the same effect. Surgery can help some puppies with valve or septal defects, but not all. Many of these puppies will have shortened life spans.

Breed Predispositions

Some breeds of dogs are at higher risk for certain heart defects. Mixed-breed puppies of those breeds also have the higher risk. In addition, heart defects can show up at random in any puppy. Having parents who have had heart screenings helps lower the risk for your pup.

German Shepherd Dogs and Poodles are at higher risk for PDA, while Newfoundlands have a higher risk of pulmonic stenosis and SAS. Golden Retrievers can be at risk for SAS. Great Danes and German Shepherd Dogs have a higher risk for valve defects, and Samoyeds and Bulldogs have a higher risk for septal defects.

Higher risk does not mean that all puppies of those breeds or mixes will have heart problems. It does mean that puppy wellness exams are very important for those pups—especially having the veterinarian do a thorough cardiac exam.

Orthopedic Problems for Small Puppies

Orthopedic problems can show up in puppies of all sizes. Some problems are caused by trauma, such as slipping on ice or leaping off the couch. Other problems are congenital (meaning present at birth). These defects in bones or joints that a puppy is born with may be genetic or may be random.

Trauma

Small-breed puppies tend to have small bones. In some cases, those thin bones are attached to long legs. A good example is an Italian Greyhound or Whippet puppy. They have long legs that are quite thin and small. Some mixed-breed puppies have similar conformation. Italian Greyhound puppies are also very, very active. They are notorious for leaping off furniture, and sometimes a broken leg will result. Other puppies are equally wild. Your Chihuahua mix may be convinced that he can fly!

If your puppy of any breed or mix cries after a crazy leap and holds his leg up, you need to visit your veterinarian. Radiographs (x-rays) will be required if she suspects a fracture. Luckily, many puppy fractures can be splinted or put in a cast and will heal nicely. Growth plate injuries, which can be quite serious, are more common with large-breed puppies.

Puppies of any size should always be under close supervision due to the risk of trauma. Never leave your puppy alone on a couch, bed, or grooming table. Discourage the puppy from jumping off a deck or down steps or out of the car. If you have to, carry him to prevent him jumping!

The Orthopedic Foundation for Animals (offa.org) keeps records on all dogs that have been screened for a potential genetic problem. They now cover many genetic defects, not just orthopedic ones. All normal results are automatically posted. Abnormal results are posted only with owner permission. You can search for a puppy's parents on the website to look for health screenings.

Luxating Patellas

The patella is the kneecap. Luxating means that instead of staying where it belongs, going straight down the rear leg from the knee joint, the patella slips to one side or the other. In toy and miniature breeds and small mixed-breed puppies, it is most common for the patella to slip medially—to the inside of the leg. This defect can be noticed as early as eight weeks of age.

Once the patella has slipped out of place, the puppy can't really bend his leg. You may notice him sort of "skipping" along, barely touching the toes of that leg to the ground. Periodically, the leg will be stretched enough that the patella slips back in place. When that happens, the puppy moves normally again.

Long-term luxated patellas lead to permanent changes in the muscles and the shape of the rear leg. In cases where both patellas are involved, both rear legs will be abnormal. Eventually arthritis will develop due to the abnormal gait and leg shape.

Your veterinarian can diagnose a luxated patella at a young age by careful palpation of the knee joint. Surgery can then be done to keep the patella in place. There are different grades of luxation, depending on how far the patella moves, how easily it returns to its normal location, and if any arthritis or defects are found. Mild cases may not need any surgery but can be managed with exercise and careful weight control.

Many breeds require certification of the patellas as part of the health screenings for those breeds. Always ask to see the certification on patellas if you purchase a small-breed puppy. Reputable breeders will have done the screening on the parents—reducing the chances of your puppy having this defect. A veterinarian does a careful palpation of both knee joints to be sure the patellas stay in place for a screening test. Only dogs with normal patellas should be bred.

Pomeranians and Yorkshire Terriers are at high risk for this problem, along with Cocker Spaniels and a number of other Terrier and toy breed dogs. Mixes of these breeds will also be at higher risk.

Legg-Calves-Perthes

Often abbreviated as Legg-Perthes or LCP, Legg-Calves-Perthes is an orthopedic condition mainly seen in toy and miniature-breed dogs, along with small Terriers. The condition is caused by a disruption in the normal blood flow to the bone of the femoral head in the hip joint.

With LCP, a young dog will have a crisis due to the lack of blood flow to the hip joint. Bone cells in the femoral head will die off. This is followed by a repair growth of blood vessels, but the damage is already done. The repaired bone is often misshapen. The joint is no longer a smooth ball and socket. Arthritis, stiffness, and pain follow.

This condition is usually evident by the time a puppy is 4 to 12 months old. An astute owner may simply notice that the pup's gait is not normal. Some puppies will carry the leg up due to pain. Others fuss only if the joint is manipulated. Muscles of an affected leg will atrophy due to lack of use.

Your veterinarian may suspect LCP simply from palpating your pup's leg and watching him move. Most dogs have only one leg affected, so the contrast between the legs helps in the diagnosis. She will use x-rays to diagnose for certain.

This condition is felt to be a genetic problem, though environmental events may influence its development. Certainly trauma to the joint could cause these signs. Yorkshire Terriers are the most commonly affected breed, but many toy and Terrier breeds may also have LCP. Due to the concerns about inheritance, dogs who have been diagnosed with LCP should not be bred. This problem is screened for by reputable breeders and certification is done through the Orthopedic Foundation for Animals.

Surgery is the recommended treatment for LCP. While it sounds drastic, the removal of the damaged femoral head leaves the puppy virtually pain free and able to lead a normal life. Families should be prepared to do follow-up rehabilitation to help the muscles rebuild on the damaged leg.

Orthopedic Problems for Big Puppies

Big puppies are the lovable but klutzy kids of the dog world. They galump instead of canter, boing instead of bounce, and trip over their feet. It may appear that a large puppy's bones have outgrown his nerves so his feet don't know what to do! These crashes can injure growing joints.

Trauma

Trauma can be more of a problem for a large-breed puppy than for a small one. Broken bones are a possibility, especially with the speed some puppies have. Hitting the deck in an uncontrolled slide or attempting to leap over the fence with unbridled enthusiasm can lead to fractures. Even roughhousing with another good-sized dog could lead to injury.

Large puppies are more prone to growth plate injuries as well as fractures. The added weight pounding when a big pup leaps and lands hard can damage the delicate areas at the ends of his long bones where growth occurs. When a growth plate is injured, the bone will not grow out to its normal length. The puppy could end up with one front leg longer than the other, for example. If the difference is significant, this causes pain and an abnormal gait. Surgery might be required.

You need to be the referee for your large puppy. Don't let him do any extra jumping until at least 1 year of age. Control his exercise—keeping him on lead if need be. He will need exercise, but you want it to be reasonable in duration and type. Swimming can be excellent for these big puppies, as they get worn out with minimal stress on their joints.

Hip Dysplasia

Those words strike fear into the hearts of big puppy owners. While mild cases of hip dysplasia may not affect your pup at all, severe cases require surgery and changes in lifestyle.

Hip dysplasia is a condition with less than ideal hip joint conformation. Any laxity or abnormality that damages the cartilage in the joint will lead to arthritis over time. Puppies with severe cases will have abnormal movement and pain from early on. Surgery may be the only option for a relatively pain-free life for a very dysplastic pup.

If you notice your puppy holding a rear leg up, being uncomfortable when sitting, or becoming less active, he may have a hip problem. Muscle atrophy in one rear leg is also a warning sign. Your veterinarian may be able to palpate laxity or may need an x-ray to be sure. If caught early, diet changes, supplements, and a set exercise regimen may help.

Puppies with mild cases of hip dysplasia can often lead normal lives with care. Keeping their weight down, giving joint supplements, and doing sensible exercise to keep muscles toned can help.

If you are getting a purebred or designer-breed puppy, look for reputable breeders who have had the hips on the parent dogs checked. They should show you an OFA certificate or you should be able to look up the parents online. Ideally you want parents with Good or Excellent hips. That is still not a guarantee of good hips, but it puts you off to a good start.

Regulate your big puppy's exercise. He needs moderate activity. Discourage jumping and wild running with turns and flips. Keep your pup's weight at an ideal level. Extra weight can influence hip conformation. Measure his meals carefully—don't just eyeball it. Your veterinarian can help you with weight-loss suggestions if your pup is chubby. Consider adding a joint supplement to your pup's diet.

Elbow Dysplasia

The phrase "elbow dysplasia" covers three possible defects involving the elbow joint of the front legs. Two of the defects arise from problems with bones in the joint and one from a problem with the cartilage in the joint. The problems may show up separately or together. The defects lead to arthritic changes in the joints, causing pain and limited range of movement.

A pup with elbow dysplasia may have an obvious limp—favoring one front leg over the other. If both elbows are affected, the pup may simply show a very shortened stride. An x-ray is used for diagnosis. Both elbows should be checked, though only one may have the defect. Surgery may be necessary for many puppies with elbow dysplasia to have normal, pain-free movement.

The four most common breeds with elbow dysplasia are all big, active breeds: Rottweilers, German Shepherd Dogs, Golden Retrievers, and Labrador Retrievers. With these pups, and any mixes of these breeds, it is important to follow sensible orthopedic precautions. Limit the jumping and high-speed turns and twists. Regulate exercise—on-lead hikes and swimming are excellent ways to wear him out. Watch his weight—those extra pounds represent more stress on his joints. If you are adding a purebred large-breed pup to your family, ask to see elbow clearances from OFA on his parents. Having clear parents is not a guarantee of no elbow problems, but it greatly increases your odds for healthy joints.

Panosteitis

If your pup is lame one day, then normal, then lame the next day but on a different leg, he may be suffering from *panosteitis*, meaning "inflammation of all bones." Puppies from 5 months to a year are most commonly affected. German Shepherd Dogs and shepherd mixes are the most likely to have this problem.

Panosteitis can be very painful, and your puppy may cry if you touch the sore leg. Some puppies will stop eating, run a fever, and may stop playing and running. Panosteitis is diagnosed by x-rays. Most puppies respond to anti-inflammatories and pain medications. Luckily, panosteitis is a problem that the puppy will outgrow, though it may take weeks or months.

Osteochondritis Dissecans, or OCD

Osteochondritis dissecans is an inflammation of the cartilage in joints. Usually when two bones meet, there is a cartilage cushion to prevent pain. If the joint cartilage is damaged or inflamed, the joint will hurt. Over time, arthritic changes take place in that joint, leading to more pain and lameness.

OCD can occur in any joint in any dog. It is most common in medium to large dogs, with the problem usually showing up in puppies between 4 and 10 months. The most common joint for this problem is the shoulder, but it can also show up in the hock, knee, or elbow. Your pup will show lameness depending on which joint and which leg is involved. Bilateral involvement, say of both shoulders, could show up as a very short stride and pain if you try to extend the puppy's legs.

This defect is diagnosed by x-ray. Surgery is often required to provide a pain-free life and minimize the development of arthritis.

It is felt that there is a genetic component to OCD, but this is another case where trauma can be involved. Energetic big-breed puppies can damage joints by rowdy play. As with other orthopedic problems, keeping your pup trim and monitoring his exercise are your best bets for avoiding this complication.

Lifestyle Considerations

Where your puppy lives and his activities can influence his health. Different environments expose your pup to different dangers. You can control some risks; others may require proactive actions by you.

A puppy exposed to secondhand smoke has a higher risk for respiratory infections and lung cancer. Leaving alcohol or prescription medications where your puppy can find them could be deadly. Those are hazards you control.

City vs. Country

Puppies face different hazards depending on where they live. A city pup who gets his exercise at the dog park or walking in parks where many dogs roam will be exposed to more parasites and diseases. He will need proper vaccinations and regular treatment for internal parasites.

Getting his proper amount of exercise means that you will get plenty of exercise, too. You need to be alert that he doesn't get into trash. In hot weather, the heat of paved surfaces can burn the pads on his paws. And salt used for melting ice and snow is a concern in cold weather.

Puppies in the country have the risk of exposure to wildlife that may carry diseases or parasites. The temptation to let your pup run loose in fields could lead to being hit by a car or attacked by a predator. You need to be careful of what your puppy finds in the country, too. Porcupines, skunks, and rodent poisons are hazards. Loose puppies and livestock can be a deadly combination.

In suburbs with a fenced yard, many families get lax about housetraining, playing with, and exercising their puppies. Your pup needs you out there with him—even in bad weather.

Where You Live

The region of the country you live in can present special health hazards. Southern California dog owners are aware of Valley Fever. Plague can be found in fleas in the Southwest. Histoplasmosis occurs in the Ohio Valley areas. Lyme disease is more common in the Northeast.

Each region has its own hazards. You need to work with your veterinarian to develop a customized health plan for your puppy. Look at disease prevalence for things like Lyme disease and leptospirosis to decide whether your pup needs those vaccines. If you travel with your puppy or are a "snowbird," you need to think about multiple regions. Partner up with your veterinarian, do some research, and plan the best way to keep your pup safe and healthy.

Your Activities

One of the best things about dogs is that they want to be with you. A well-trained dog can accompany you in many places. Your puppy may lead you to some new activities, too.

Dogs are great hiking companions. Hiking has some risks, however. Lakes and ponds may be filled with giardia parasites. Carrying fresh drinking water is important for your pup and you.

Many puppies will eventually be great jogging or running partners. You need to be cautious about over-stressing your pup, though. Puppies do their best to stay with you—pushing themselves beyond sensible limits for their growing joints. Be considerate of your puppy's limitations. Think about the weather and the surfaces you are asking your pup to walk over.

Swimming is wonderful exercise for you and your pup. If you swim in a lake or pond, remember to bring drinking water. Keep in mind that, just like with running, your puppy may not be sensible about when to stop.

If you have a pool, gate it off so your puppy can't access it without you. Add a ramp so the pup could climb out if he fell in.

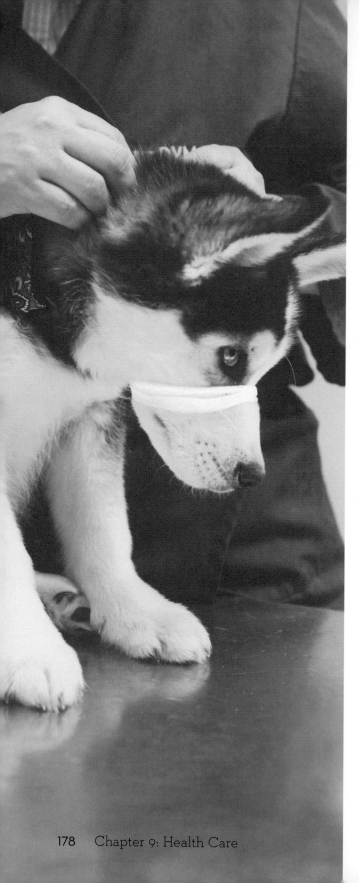

Emergencies: First Aid and Poison Control

Emergency care is just that: what you do in a crisis, followed by veterinary backup. Basic first aid principles are the same for people and pets. Thoroughly puppy-proofing your home can prevent many emergencies.

Important Rules for All Emergencies

One of the most important rules is to stay calm. If you panic, you won't think clearly, and you will convey your anxiety to your puppy. Many emergencies require a trip to the veterinarian after initial care. Use a crate for transport if possible, or have a friend drive while you hold the puppy. Know where your nearest emergency clinic is ahead of time in case your regular clinic is closed.

Even the sweetest puppy may bite if he is frightened or hurting. Small puppies can be wrapped in a towel. A larger pup might need a muzzle. You can purchase a muzzle at a pet supply store, or fashion a quick one at home with a roll of gauze or a scarf.

Make a loop and put it around your pup's muzzle. He will be able to breathe fine through his nose. Then tie a bow or loop behind his ears. Dogs with short muzzles are best simply wrapped in a towel.

Bleeding Injuries

A puppy may cut himself on a dropped knife, get a bite wound from another animal, or run into a tree branch. These situations could lead to a bleeding wound. Apply pressure to the wound. If blood is spurting, an artery is cut. Unless it is a major artery, he is not in immediate danger of bleeding out, but he will require veterinary attention.

Do not use a tourniquet unless you have had training. In most cases, direct pressure will stop the bleeding. Pressure with a cold pack wrapped in a cloth is even more effective. Small wounds can be bandaged, but larger ones may require sutures. Once the bleeding is stopped or slowing, apply gauze pads and wrap the area with a gauze roll to hold the pads in place.

CPR for Puppies

CPR stands for *cardio* (heart), *pulmonary* (lungs), and *resuscitation*. CPR can be done for puppies, but with care. First, feel for a heartbeat. If the heart is beating, you don't need compressions. If there is no heartbeat, lay your puppy down on his right side. You can put very small puppies in your palm and gently squeeze in from behind the elbows. For larger pups, compress gently inward behind the elbow.

Figure one breath into the nose with the mouth held closed for every five compressions. This is easiest if you have help, but you can do it yourself. Check periodically to see if the puppy is breathing on his own and has a heartbeat. You can sign up for pet first aid and CPR courses at many Red Cross offices.

Be prepared to accept the reality that if your pup is so badly injured as to need CPR, you may not be able to revive him. Head to your veterinary clinic as soon as possible.

Electrical Shocks

Puppies are attracted to electrical cords. Sometimes they chew a cord because it looks fun to tug on. You have to stay uninjured to help your pup. First, pull the plug from the wall. If the wires are chewed and are sparking, use a wooden implement to do that. Once the current is off, check your puppy for a heartbeat. Do CPR if needed. Check the mouth for electrical burns. Lift the lips and look at the gums. Take him to your veterinarian for a thorough evaluation.

Vomiting and Diarrhea

Stomach and intestinal upsets can be life threatening in a puppy due to their small size. A puppy dehydrates faster than an adult dog. If your pup vomits once and there is no blood, and he is acting fine otherwise, observe carefully. Make sure he has water, but pick up any food. If he cannot keep water down, he needs to go to the veterinary clinic.

If he keeps water down, try offering frequent but very small, bland meals. A tablespoon, or teaspoon for a tiny pup, of canned fish or chicken, boiled rice, or boiled hamburger is generally well accepted. Do not give any medications without consulting your veterinarian first—even over-the-counter remedies.

If your pup vomits more than once, vomits up blood, has blood in diarrhea, or the vomit is accompanied by diarrhea, he needs a veterinarian. Do not offer food but try to give water while you head to the clinic.

Choking

Choking is one case where you may be able to handle an emergency by yourself. If you notice your pup gagging, coughing, or turning blue, he may have something stuck in an upper airway. Look in his mouth. Common problems are a ball stuck in the back of the mouth or a stick across the roof of the mouth. You may be able to pull out a stick or a ball. The stick is not an immediate emergency; your pup can breathe around it.

The ball is another story. If you can't grab and remove it, tip your pup upside down while you support him. Another option is the canine version of the Heimlich maneuver. Give a squeeze upwards with a balled fist behind your pup's ribcage. This should be done quickly to give thrust. If you can't move it, shift the ball so there is some air flow and head for the veterinary clinic.

Seizures

Minor seizures might just involve the muscles of one leg and appear as tremors. What we tend to think of as seizures are grand mal seizures. In those cases, your pup loses consciousness and collapses. His legs may paddle, he may drool, and he may urinate or defecate. These seizures are generally very short. Afterward, your pup may be dazed for a short time but then act as if nothing happened.

If your pup has a seizure, do not panic. He can't swallow his tongue. Do not put your hand in his mouth, as he may bite you unintentionally. Keep him quiet—wrap him in a blanket if you need to. Take him to the veterinary clinic even if the seizure has ended. You may find the cause if blood work is done immediately. However, many seizures are caused by a genetic predisposition or have unknown causes.

Poisonings

Poisonings are a common emergency in puppies. Puppies use their mouths to explore their world. Almost anything they are interested in gets picked up and chewed on.

The most common poisonings are from human medications. If you drop a pill on the floor, your pup may snag it and swallow it. A pill bottle may look like a toy to play with. While chewing on it, your puppy may swallow some pills. Some medications and food additives that are safe for people, like the sweetener xylitol, are toxic to dogs.

If your pup has gotten into something and you aren't sure if it is toxic, call your veterinarian or one of the animal poison control centers. They can tell you if you need to be concerned and what treatment is best. For many items, having your pup vomit it back up right away is ideal. That can be done with a dose of hydrogen peroxide.

Some toxins are best left to pass through. Treatments like giving an activated charcoal slurry may be suggested. Always check before trying any therapy on your own.

There are two national pet poison control hotlines:

ASPCA Animal Poison Control
aspca.org/pet-care/ animal-poison-control at 888-426-4435

Pet Poison Hotline
petpoisonhelpline.com/poisons/ at 800-231-6680.

Thinking Ahead: Microchipping and Pet Insurance

"Be prepared" is the perfect motto for puppy owners. To help you prepare for emergencies, microchip your pup and sign up for pet health insurance.

Microchips

Your pup may already have a microchip implanted by his breeder, shelter, or rescue group.

A microchip is a small identification capsule the size of a rice grain. It is injected under the puppy's skin. This may cause a second or two of pain, but it immediately goes away.

When read with a scanner, the microchip provides a number that has been uniquely assigned to your puppy. Most veterinary clinics and animal shelters have scanners available.

A microchip provides two things. First, it identifies your puppy. If your puppy is lost and is picked up by animal control, dropped off at an animal shelter, or taken to a veterinary hospital, he can be identified. The presence of a microchip suggests that this is someone's pet, not a homeless stray.

Secondly, the microchip can be used to prove that this is your puppy. With the paperwork proving that you own this pup, you should have no trouble reclaiming him. A microchip is important even if you plan to have ID tags on your puppy's collar. When dogs get lost, many manage to lose their collars. Dogs with microchips are much more likely to be returned to their owners.

Both of the big advantages of microchipping require that you register the microchip and your pup with an identification service. The companies that make and register microchips have no idea which puppy they will be used for until you return the forms. Once your forms are returned, the companies provide a 24/7 phone line. If your puppy is found, the microchip is scanned. The company is contacted and they will have your contact information available. Update your information if you move or get a new phone number or email account.

Pet Health Insurance

Veterinary medicine has made major strides forward in recent decades. With the medical advances have come increased costs. You don't want your care decisions to be influenced by economics if at all possible.

This is where pet health insurance comes in. Pet policies can be set up for a wide range of coverage. Most policies are much less expensive if you register a puppy as opposed to an adult dog.

Pet health policies fall into two areas. One set of policies covers routine care and wellness plans. A policy like that pays benefits for regular veterinary visits and preventive care. More commonly, policies are set to cover major accidents such as a broken leg or major illnesses, such as cancer requiring chemotherapy. Some pet owners choose to cover both.

The cost of a policy varies with the deductible and how much coverage you want. Many families budget for routine care but want a backup for a major problem. In general, pre-existing conditions are not covered, so it makes sense to sign up your pup and not wait for problems to appear. Companies may have certain conditions they will not cover.

Research pet health insurance companies. Read the fine print and look at what conditions are and are not covered. Decide how much of a deductible you can handle. See if the company your microchip is registered with offers a companion pet health insurance policy. That may cut costs even more.

Chapter 10

Training Basics

- Punishment versus reward, and how to get started with positive training
- Teaching your puppy to behave everywhere
- Foundational commands

Whether or not you are doing it consciously, every interaction you have with your puppy is training. The puppy is learning something. People often think of training as something formal in which your goal is to teach the puppy a behavior such as sit. However, the puppy doesn't stop learning when you aren't in training mode.

It is easy to make excuses for puppies and allow them to get away with behaviors we would not tolerate in an adult dog. Think of this from the pup's perspective. If you allow him to do something now, he will assume it is okay. If you correct him for the same behavior later, he is going to be very confused. The longer you allow an unwanted behavior to go on, the longer it is going to take to fix it.

Training also helps exercise your puppy's mind, which is just as important as exercising his body. Many dogs were bred originally to have a job, such as herding sheep. Most dogs now just live in our homes and provide companionship. Yet the dog's intellect is still in place. He needs something to do with his brain, and training can provide just that.

Don't think of training as a chore; instead make it fun for both you and the pup. There is no right or wrong thing to train your puppy to do. If you don't care about sit or down, don't teach them. If teaching your puppy to walk on a loose leash is important, train that first. Read the sections on positive training, using cues, and identifying rewards before you start training any of the behaviors in this chapter.

Punishment Versus Rewards

Some people think of punishment in terms of actually hitting the dog or forcing him to do something. However, punishment is anything the puppy finds unpleasant or scary. Many people know that choke chains, prong collars, and electric collars fall into the punishment category. But squirting a puppy with water or shaking a can of pennies if he does something wrong are things many owners think are okay. Both can still be very punishing to the puppy. Even jerking your puppy hard on his leash while he is wearing a flat-buckle collar could be stressful. It all depends on the puppy and how he takes the action.

Because punishment has been something people have used for training for so long, the American Veterinary Society of Animal Behavior has put out position statements for veterinarians and other animal professionals stating why punishment should not be used for training. The AVSAB reports that using punishment for behavior problems could have many adverse effects, such as inhibition of learning, and increased fear-related and aggressive behaviors.

Punishment may stop a behavior initially, but it doesn't fix the reason you were punishing the puppy. The punishment may also inhibit the puppy and stop him from showing more signs of stress. A puppy that is stressed but is hiding that stress could end up biting at some point.

For example, if the puppy was nipping you and you decided to grab his muzzle and shake it, he most likely would initially stop biting and back up. He would not understand you were shaking his muzzle because he was biting you. Instead, he would become nervous when he saw your hand approaching his face (such as it would do if you were going to pet him or leash him). The puppy may decide to start biting any hands that come near him.

Choke chains, prong collars, and electric training collars can also injure the dog, especially in the hands of a novice trainer.

One of the biggest reasons not to use punishment is it can damage the bond between you and your puppy. If your dog becomes afraid of you, not only may he avoid you, but any issues you already had will become worse. At some point the punishment or threat of punishment could lead the dog to bite you.

Rewarding your puppy with treats, praise, or a toy will cause him to love training with you. Instead of being worried about your next action, the puppy will run up to you and give you his attention, hoping you will interact with him.

Four Types of Learning

Trainers often break learning into the following areas:

Positive Reinforcement: If you give the puppy something he wants when he performs a behavior, you increase the likelihood he will offer the behavior again. For example, if the puppy loves chicken and you give him a bite of chicken every time he sits, you will increase the likelihood the puppy will sit again.

Negative Reinforcement: If you remove something aversive, you increase the likelihood of a behavior happening again. For example, if you push down on the puppy's butt to make him sit, and immediately release the pressure when he sits, he may sit to avoid the discomfort of having his butt pushed down.

Positive Punishment: By adding something the puppy dislikes, you will decrease the likelihood he will perform the behavior again. For example, if your puppy tries to jump up on you and you push him down with your hand, he may stop jumping to avoid the punishment.

Negative Punishment: By ignoring behavior you do not want from the puppy, you decrease the likelihood that he will repeat that behavior. If he jumps up on you, turning away from him and taking away your attention tells him there is no game, and he will be less likely to do this in the future.

For the purposes of this book, all of our training will involve either positive reinforcement or negative punishment. We will either reward the puppy for doing something we want or remove something (such as our attention) for actions we don't want.

Identifying Rewards

Before you start training, you need to identify ways to pay your dog. Many people use dog treats, some people use the dog's dry kibble, and others use meat or toys. Whatever you use, it has to be something the dog wants.

Finding Treats Your Puppy Wants Most

Not all dog treats are created equal. Shop around and find one or two that your dog really enjoys. One thing to keep in mind is that a treat your dog enjoys when he is in your home with nothing else going on may not be a good treat to use in the classroom or outside where there are more distractions. Sometimes you have to increase the value of the reward in order to keep the dog's attention.

Many people use hot dogs or cooked chicken as training treats. Chicken can be especially good for dogs who have sensitive stomachs.

Once you have identified the rewards your dog finds most valuable, use them only when training. If you want to give your dog a treat because he is cute or you love him, use a less valuable reward. You want the puppy to figure out that the only way to get the thing he wants most in the world is to do what you ask him to do.

When using food as a reward, keep the treat size small. You do not want your puppy to get fat. A treat the size of a small eraser is generally about right. When you are training and your puppy is getting a lot of treats, cut back on the amount of kibble he gets that day to help keep him at a good weight.

Using Toys as Rewards

Some dogs may do better working for a toy rather than food. If your dog loves toys, especially tennis balls or tug toys, do some experiments and see if he prefers toys or food as a reward. Some dogs need variety, and what works one day may not work the next, so be creative.

Ranking Treats by Their Value to Your Puppy

Identify a variety of things your dog will work for and rank them in order of importance. When you are training something new or working in a distracting environment, bring out the best rewards. Once your dog begins to know a cue or is working in a less distracting environment, you may be able to use a less valuable reward.

Treat Bags

Because you will want to get to your rewards quickly, you need a treat bag. Most commercial treat bags are designed to keep the treats at waist level so you can access them quickly. Find one that is easy to clean.

A complaint often heard from owners when using food as a reward is that they will have to carry the food around forever. Many savvy trainers actually do keep food with them most of the time because they know their dog is always learning. You never know when a training opportunity may arise. But if you don't want to carry food with you, you won't have to. The goal is to get to the point where you will ask your puppy for a behavior without the food being present. However, you must always pay your puppy for doing something you ask him to do. That payment doesn't have to be just food. You could pay your puppy by saying "good dog" or scratching him under the chin.

Positive Training

There are many different types of training. Most of what you will be trying in this book will fall under either lure and reward–based training or clicker training. These are both considered positive dog training methods.

Lure and Reward Training

In lure training, you use the reward to lure the dog into the position you want and then give him the reward. For example, if you were teaching sit, you would put the treat just above the dog's nose, and as he reached up and back to get the treat, his butt would begin to drop and he would get the treat.

Clicker Training

A clicker is a device that makes a distinct noise when a button is pushed. Once a dog understands clicker training, he knows the clicker marks a behavior and he is going to be paid for doing that behavior. The clicker is highly effective because dogs have a very narrow association window. This means that you have one or two seconds to give your dog a reward for him to understand why he is getting that reward.

With the clicker, you can teach the dog that whatever he was doing at the exact moment you clicked was correct and that payment is coming. In addition to marking the behavior, the clicker gives you a little extra time to deliver your payment because the clicker acts as a contract, and your puppy will learn a reward will always follow that sound.

Advantages and Disadvantages of Both Training Types

There are advantages and disadvantages to both types of training. In lure training, people often use food to lure a puppy too long. The puppy quickly decides that if he doesn't see the treat, he isn't going to perform the action. To effectively use a lure, you need to use the food a few times, and then use only the motion of the lure and pay the dog after he performs. Clicker training is all about timing, and you need to learn to click right when you see the behavior you want to mark.

Getting Started with Clicker Training

The first step in clicker training is to teach your dog the click has meaning and that the click will always be followed by a reward. A clicker is not a remote control. It is not used to get your dog's attention or call the dog to you. The click marks a very precise behavior and tells the dog he is being rewarded for that precise behavior.

Obviously, dogs are not born understanding clickers. You have to teach them. One easy way to get started with clicker training is to put 10 treats in a bowl. Click and then immediately give your dog one reward. Repeat until all 10 treats are gone. Refill your bowl with 10 more treats. Wait for your dog to turn his head away from you, then click. If the dog looks back at you, he is beginning to understand that the sound of the click means payment is coming. If he doesn't look back, go through your next 10 treats by just clicking and handing the dog a treat.

If your pup seems afraid of the noise of the clicker, muffle the noise by holding the clicker behind your back. Once he begins to realize the click is followed by an awesome reward, he will generally become less afraid of the noise.

Clicker Training Exercises

There are two very simple exercises to teach your dog that clicker training is fun and to help you with your timing.

Hand Targeting

The first is to teach the puppy to target your hand. You will need your puppy on a leash, your clicker, and your treats. Start in an area free of distractions.

1. Place your hand right in front of your pup's nose. Most puppies will reach out and touch something right in front of them. The minute your pup touches your fingers or your palm, click and treat. The clicker should not be in the hand the puppy is touching.

2. Start with your hand very close to your pup's nose. If he doesn't touch the hand right away, take it away quickly and then try again. Eventually he will figure out that touching your hand makes a reward happen and he will begin to understand that the click sounded just as he touched your hand.

If you click, *always* treat, even if you didn't mean to click. You need your puppy to understand the rules will always be the same. Do not have the food in your hand when you are using the clicker. The puppy needs to think that the reward only happens after he hears the click and not be focused on where the food is. Keep your hand out of your treat bag until after you click.

Once your puppy reliably understands a cue for a behavior, you can stop clicking. The click is only to teach the behavior.

3. As your puppy gets better at the game, give it a name such as "touch." You would add the cue right as he touches your hand.

4. After the puppy is touching your hand repeatedly while it is just inches from his nose, move your hand farther away and say "touch." If the pup comes forward and touches your hand, click and give him lots of treats and verbal praise. If the pup doesn't come forward, move your hand close to his nose again and keep working.

Stepping onto a Mat

Another easy game is to teach your puppy to step onto a mat. The mat can be anything from a towel to a dog bed. Have your puppy on a leash if necessary, get your mat, and go to a quiet spot.

1. Place the mat on the floor and quietly stare at it as if it is the most interesting thing in the world. Keep your pup's leash short if you are using one, so she doesn't have much room to investigate. Soon she will come and look at the mat. Begin by just clicking and treating if she touches the mat with any part of her body.

2. As she begins to understand that the click has something to do with the mat, wait for her to put more of herself on the mat and then click for that.

Be sure to pick up the mat when you aren't playing this game so the pup won't accidently step on it and not get a reward. Both hand targeting and the mat can be used as building blocks for numerous other behaviors.

3. Eventually the pup will have all four feet on the mat. When that happens, show her a treat and throw the treat off to the side. Do not click when you throw the treat. The pup will run and get the treat, which resets her so you can continue the game. You want to give her more treats for being on the mat than the single treat she will get for going off the matt. Soon you will be playing a game where she runs and gets on the mat whenever she sees it.

Using Cues

A cue is a word that a person associates with an action the puppy performs. For example "sit" is the cue most often used when the puppy puts her butt on the ground.

People become very frustrated with their dogs because they appear to not always listen to cues. The owner generally attributes this to the puppy being stubborn, when in reality the puppy may never have understood the word, or may not understand the word in a new context.

Puppies do not generalize. This means that if you only taught your puppy to sit while you were sitting in a chair in the living room, she may not sit if you are standing up outside. She would not understand the word means the same thing in this different context.

Humans also start attaching cues to behaviors before the puppy is actually offering the behavior. This can be very confusing to the puppy. If you start saying "sit" and she has no idea what that means, by the time she figures out she is getting a treat for putting her butt on the ground, "sit" may be just meaningless background noise.

Achieving Consistency

Do not give an action a cue until the puppy is performing that action at least 80 percent of the time. If your puppy sits 80 percent of the time while you are working with her, start to add the cue "sit" right as her butt goes down. Then you would say "sit" slightly earlier. Next you would start to say the cue before the action started to see if she understands that is the word that means put your butt on the floor.

Always start working on a new behavior in a quiet area. Once she knows the word in the least distracting environment, start training the behavior in a new location. If she doesn't do the behavior on cue in the new location, go back to targeting or luring her for a few repetitions. Soon she will learn that the word has the same meaning everywhere she hears it.

Once you are sure your puppy understands a cue, reward her only when you ask for the behavior. If you reward her when she offers the behavior but you didn't ask for it, she will go through her life throwing behaviors at you trying to see which one you might be paying for.

Never say your cue more than once. Humans get in the habit of repeating a cue over and over and then rewarding the puppy when she finally does it. You need her to understand she will get a reward only when she performs the behavior the very first time you ask.

Distance and Distractions

Distance and distractions are the cause of many issues in training. A puppy may learn to sit but can only do the behavior when you are within 1 foot (30.5cm) of her. That is because most people train the behavior only when they are standing right in front of the puppy. If you want your puppy to be able to sit when you are several feet away, you gradually have to increase the distance between you and the puppy while asking for the sit.

Puppies also often learn things in context. If you teach your puppy to sit while you are standing right in front of her, then go for a walk and ask her to sit right beside you, chances are good she will run in front of you, stop, and sit. She thinks "sit" means being in front of you. You actually have to teach the puppy to sit beside you as well as in front of you.

When you add distractions, start with the distraction far away and gradually move closer as the puppy begins to understand that your game is the same no matter what is going on around her.

Teaching Waiting at Doors

Distractions can cause your puppy to bolt out the door anytime it is opened. It is far safer to teach your puppy to wait while you open a door. Also teach the puppy to wait before she comes out of her crate and before she gets out of a vehicle. To start, you will need treats, a door, your clicker, and your puppy on a leash. Do not let her off leash until you are confident in this behavior. Do not teach your puppy this behavior if you still have housebreaking issues.

1. Place your hand on the door. If the puppy rushes forward, take your hand away. If she backs away from the door, even if only an inch, click and treat. Repeat until you can touch the door without her rushing forward.

2. Begin to push the door open. If the puppy rushes forward, close the door and wait for her to back up, then click and treat. If she doesn't rush the door, reward her. Repeat until you can push the door slightly open without her rushing forward.

3. As soon as she is backing away or standing still when the door is slightly open, give her a cue that you are going outside. As soon as you open the door a crack and the puppy is giving you a behavior you like, open the door all the way and immediately say "Let's go" to indicate it is okay to go out the door, and go out with her.

4. Come back inside. Open the door wider and click and treat for either standing still or backing away from the door. If she rushes toward the door, close it. Repeat until she is standing at the door without rushing forward while you open it.

5. As soon as she is beginning to back up a bit from the door or stand by your side, give this a cue such as "Wait." Begin to pair the cue "Wait" with "Let's go."

6. Practice opening the door wider and wider, asking the puppy to "Wait" until you give her the cue "Let's go."

7. Ask her to wait and do not give her the cue to go out the door. Instead go outside without her. If she starts to follow you, stop, go back in, and wait for her to back up from the door.

8. Alternate between allowing her to go out with you on the cue "Let's go" and going out the door without her. You want the puppy to understand that sometimes you will say "Wait" and she will stay behind.

Furniture Etiquette

Whether or not to allow the puppy on the furniture is a personal choice, and there is no right or wrong answer. But don't make your decision based on inaccurate information. Your dog will not dominate you if you allow her to be on your couch or to sleep on your bed. It is perfectly fine for your puppy to be on your furniture as long as it's okay with you.

If you do not want your puppy on the furniture, then from the moment you bring her home begin teaching her the floor is an awesome place to be. It isn't fair to the puppy to allow her on the furniture when she is small and then one day decide she is now too big to be on it.

If you want your puppy to stay on the floor, place a bed or blanket near all of the places you will be sitting. Your puppy will want to be near the action. Whenever she comes near you while you are sitting on the couch or your favorite chair, give her something of high value to chew on when she steps onto the bed you have placed on the floor. Soon she will learn that sitting quietly by you is rewarding.

If your puppy is too ramped up to settle down or chew on something, put her in her crate until she calms down. Don't make her think you are angry at her before you put her in the crate, but you can use the crate as a place for the puppy to rest and chew without bothering the family.

If you constantly push the puppy off the couch or yell at her, she may think this is a great game whenever she wants you to interact with her. You need to ignore her bothering you on the couch and reward her for being on her bed near the couch. Another solution is to get up and move away anytime she jumps up on the couch, but reward her if she comes near the couch but does not jump up. This will require a lot of getting up and down on your part at first, but the puppy will soon learn that you leave and ignore her if she gets up on the couch, whereas she will get your attention or a treat if she approaches and does not jump up on the couch.

If you want to allow your puppy on the furniture sometimes, but not all the time, teach her that it's okay to get on the furniture only when she's invited. Teaching the cues "on" and "off" can be very useful when dealing with furniture issues.

While it is possible to teach your puppy not to be on the furniture when you are home, do not expect that same behavior when you are gone. If she absolutely cannot be on the furniture, be sure she is crated whenever you leave the house.

Staying Home Alone

Be sure your puppy is crate trained before you start leaving her home alone. Having a puppy that can happily stay in her crate while you are away keeps her and your home safe. If you are unable to crate your puppy, leave her in a small space free from hazards such as chemicals or power cords. Test the space first when you can be home and check on her. You want to make sure that the place you leave your puppy is indeed puppy proof.

If you live in an apartment complex or other type of housing where someone could hear your puppy if she barked, it is important to know how your puppy acts when you leave. It is always a good idea to talk to your neighbors and be proactive. Tell them you have a new puppy and that you want to make sure she is not disturbing anyone. Ask to be alerted right away if they hear your puppy barking for a prolonged period.

Generally you can discover how your puppy will be when you leave by doing a few test runs without actually leaving the vicinity of your home. Put the puppy in her crate or room. Leave her with something to do, such as a long-lasting chew or a food-dispensing toy. Walk out the door and then stop and listen. If you don't hear barking after 15 minutes, take a walk around the block. When you come back, stand outside the house and listen again. If the puppy isn't barking, chances are good she will be okay when you are gone.

As your puppy gets older and becomes reliably housebroken, you may wish to leave her loose while you are gone. Just remember, a bored puppy could decide to redecorate your home while you are gone.

It is often prudent to start by leaving the puppy loose in a small area rather than giving her the run of the house. The first time you leave your puppy alone, only do so for less than half an hour. As long as the puppy isn't destroying anything, slowly increase the time you are gone and your puppy is loose.

If the puppy does well in a small area, then you can gradually allow her more freedom in the house. Just go slow and check in on her frequently in the beginning to ensure she isn't getting into trouble. If you have more than one dog loose in the house or if your home contains other pets such as cats, it is especially important that you allow the puppy to be loose for only short amounts of time until you are confident all the animals are getting along.

If you come home to a mess of any kind, do not punish the puppy. She will not understand what she is being punished for. Instead of punishing her, figure out what happened and find a solution to prevent it from happening in the future, such as crating her or picking up things she can get into.

If your puppy is barking, see the section on barking in the next chapter.

Going for a Walk

Walks are not only great exercise, but provide an awesome opportunity to bond with your puppy. The goal of a walk is for both you and the puppy to have fun. Unfortunately, walks often turn into battlegrounds. Some puppies pull hard and drag their owners along. Others are terrified on walks and stop often. Other issues include puppies who stop to sniff every smell, or puppies who lunge and bark when they see other people or animals on a walk.

Don't fall for the old dominance myth that says never let your puppy walk in front of you. Where he walks has absolutely no bearing on his relationship with you. You and the puppy need to decide on a mutually beneficial approach to walks. Dogs naturally sniff and follow their noses. Constantly denying your pup the opportunity to explore, sniff, and pee where other dogs have peed could cause him to become frustrated. On the other hand, you do not have to live with a puppy that pulls your arm out of its socket or that stops every 10 seconds to smell something. Teaching good leash walking skills while your puppy is small will pay off later in life, especially if he will grow into a big dog.

Why Puppies Pull

To start, let's discuss why puppies pull. There are many reasons, but a big one is that the owner pays the puppy to do so. If your puppy pulls on the leash and your arm extends, he gets several feet of extra leash just for pulling. If you are using a retractable leash that allows the puppy to pull and get many feet of extra leash, he is just going to learn to pull more. Never use a retractable leash if you are trying to teach your puppy not to pull.

Many puppies pull because of the tension against their neck. They feel the pressure and pull hard against it. This is why you see so many dogs choking themselves while pulling forward. The leash and collar are doing nothing to make the pup not want to pull.

For people who don't have time for a lot of training, there are a number of amazing no-pull harnesses on the market. A no-pull harness doesn't necessarily teach your puppy not to pull, but depending on where the leash is attached or how the harness fits, it prevents the puppy from pulling so hard. For no-pull harnesses to work, they must be properly fitted and you need to spend time teaching your puppy to enjoy wearing it. For many puppies, once the pressure of a collar is gone from their neck, their pulling is greatly reduced or disappears altogether.

Let's Go

Teaching the "let's go" cue can help you when you want your puppy to move along after he has been sniffing. It is just fine to let the puppy have some fun sniffing, but you also want to have a way to tell him the sniff fest is over and it is time to move along. It is also a good idea to teach your puppy a cue such as "free dog" that means it is okay for him to take a moment and sniff.

1. When your puppy is engaged in sniffing something, call his name. If he looks back at you, say "let's go" and give him a treat when he comes away from the spot he smelled. If he doesn't look back at you when you call him, stand still and wait. Eventually he will look back at you. When he does, give him lots of praise and treats. He will soon learn that checking in with you can be more rewarding than sniffing.

2. As you are walking, when your puppy appears to be interested in going to sniff an object, stand still, wait for the puppy to look back at you, and give the cue "free dog" and allow him to move forward to sniff the object.

3. When it is time to move on, say "let's go," and reward him for coming back to you or going on with the walk.

Soon the puppy will learn that "free dog" means it is okay to stop and sniff and "let's go" indicates it is time to start moving again.

Never allow your puppy to walk in public off leash. Even if he's very good at coming back when you call him, chances are there will be something your puppy will just have to run after. Before deciding to let your puppy walk off leash, ask yourself if you are 100 percent confident you can immediately call him to you if he sees a squirrel, rabbit, or another dog. If you are not, do not let him off leash in public.

Meeting Strangers and Other Dogs

Going for a walk is also about what to do when you meet or pass other dogs or people. Puppies attract people. Do not let well-meaning strangers ruin your polite greeting. Teach your puppy to sit, or at least keep all four feet on the ground, when people want to pet him.

Teach your puppy from the very beginning that he will never go up to sniff another dog while he is out for a walk on a leash. It is very stressful for some dogs to meet another dog while both are on leash. The dogs have no way to get away from each other if they get scared. Meeting on leash forces the dogs to meet face to face. Dogs generally prefer not to meet head on.

Another reason to stop your puppy from going up to sniff other dogs is that the pup could start to anticipate the meeting and begin dragging you toward any dog he sees. While he might be okay meeting another dog, the dog he is meeting might not enjoy it.

If you teach your puppy that he will not go up and sniff other dogs, he will soon learn to ignore dogs he sees, even those that are close to him. It only takes one or two bad experiences for your puppy to become afraid when he sees other dogs when out for a walk. If he becomes too scared of seeing dogs while walking, he may start to bark and growl when he sees a dog. This will make walking him even more difficult. If you want your puppy to play with other dogs, do it in a place where the dogs can be safely off leash.

Be prepared to defend your puppy from dogs that are off leash. It can be extremely traumatic for a puppy to have a strange dog rush in and sniff him. It can also be dangerous if the dog that is loose decides to attack your puppy. If you see a loose dog, position your puppy so that you are between him and the other dog. Do anything you deem safe to stop the other dog from getting near your puppy. If the dog has an owner nearby, politely ask the owner to leash his dog and explain that your puppy is learning to not meet dogs on a walk. If the dog has no apparent owner, leave the area as soon as possible.

Heel

Teaching your puppy to heel or at least be close to your side while on a walk is also important. There will be times on your walk when you want your puppy close to you. You will need your puppy on a leash, your treats and clicker, and a distraction-free area with plenty of room for walking. You also need to determine which side the puppy will walk on. If you plan to do any formal competition work with your puppy, teach him to heel on your left side. Otherwise, it doesn't matter. If you want the puppy to walk on your right side instead, just substitute "right" when you see the word "left."

1. Fill your left hand with treats. With your puppy on your left side, show him a treat and drop it behind your left foot. Every time your left foot moves forward you will show him a treat and place it behind your left foot. It is very important that the puppy see you place the treat on the ground.

2. Once the puppy has decided being behind your left foot is fun, place the treat behind your foot on every second stride instead of every single stride. If he starts getting ahead of you, go back to putting the treat in every left footstep again.

3. Pay attention to whether your puppy starts to watch your hand place the treat on the ground. If he figures out the food is coming from your hand, go on to step 4.

4. Place a treat behind your left foot, walk forward, and see if your puppy stares at your left hand. If the puppy is walking at your side or slightly behind you and looking at your left hand, click and treat. At this point you can hand the puppy the treat if he is beside you, or continue to place it behind your left foot.

5. Move your left hand so it is at hip level. If the puppy looks at the hand, click and treat. At this point you can take the treats out of your hand and return them to your treat bag. You will reward the puppy after every click but will be reaching into the treat bag to get the treat.

6. Begin to take more and more steps before you click and treat. If your puppy remains by your side staring at your left hand, praise him. Continue this step until he is walking beside you and looking up at you for longer and longer periods.

7. If the puppy gets ahead of you, turn around and go the opposite direction. As soon as he is beside your left leg, click and treat; continue clicking and treating every step a few more times. Then go back and ask him to go for longer and longer distances between each click.

8. Once he is walking beside you looking up at you or at your left hand, give this a cue, such as "heel." When you need your puppy to be near you, use that cue. When it is okay for the puppy to go out in front of you, use "free dog" so he knows he no longer has to heel.

Going for a Car Ride

Teaching your puppy to ride in the car is fun and will provide lifelong benefits. One reason dogs grow up to be fearful about car rides is that people often take their dog only to the vet or some other stressful place. You want your puppy to assume getting in the car means a big adventure is about to happen and it will involve lots of fun and rewards. It may take you several days or even longer to get to the point where you are pulling out of your driveway.

Before you begin to work with your puppy on getting in the vehicle, decide where he will ride. It is far safer for him to be in a crate than loose. Crates can also protect your puppy if you are in an accident. Air bags can kill dogs, and they can be thrown from cars during an accident if not restrained. If a crate will not fit in your vehicle, there are several styles of seatbelts designed for dogs.

Teach your puppy that getting in the vehicle is fun. You will need high-value treats, a long leash, and your clicker. Do not train this behavior until you have taught your puppy "touch."

1. Have the puppy on a long leash so he has plenty of room to get away from the car if it frightens him.

2. Sit in the seat nearest the place where you have decided the puppy will ride. Hold the end of the leash and click and treat him if he looks toward you while you are sitting in the vehicle. If he appears nervous about the vehicle, toss the treats toward him rather than force him to come to the vehicle to receive a reward. Do not use the treats to lure the puppy to the vehicle. You want him to come closer at his own pace.

3. If the puppy happily comes up to you to get the treat, move on to the next step. If he is worried about being near the car, work on him just looking at the car and then stop and go back in the house. You want the puppy to have fun near the vehicle until he is confident coming to you while you are in the car.

4. Have the puppy target your hand near the car door, and click and treat.

5. Position your target hand so the puppy has to stretch up and move his nose into the doorway of the vehicle. Click and treat.

6. Use your target hand to get the puppy to move more and more of his body inside the vehicle. If he is too small to jump into the vehicle, use some type of platform outside the car so he can get up high enough to jump into the car. Continue to click and treat for your puppy to move farther into the car.

7. Once he is all the way inside the vehicle, stop the game and ask the puppy to get out of the car. Either call him to you or ask him to target your hand. Always click and treat if the puppy targets your hand. Take a break and play the game again until he is confident and jumping into the vehicle when he sees your hand target. At this point you can put this on cue, such as "in" or "ride."

8. As soon as the puppy is confidently jumping in and out of the vehicle, begin to put him into his crate or seatbelt. If using a seatbelt, have someone continuously feed the puppy while you fasten him in. In this way he won't become agitated about being in the seatbelt. If you are using a crate, teach him to go in the crate using the same methods you would if the crate were in the house.

Never allow your dog to stick his head out the window while you are driving. Even if the window is up far enough that the dog can't jump out, he could still be injured by debris hitting his face. Never allow your puppy to ride loose in the back of a pickup truck.

9. When the puppy is fine with getting in the vehicle and then going into his crate or being belted in, close the doors and start the engine. Have someone near the puppy who can feed him treats or use their voice to praise him for good behavior.

10. If he appears unstressed by the doors closing and the engine starting, pull out of your driveway. Immediately pull back in, get the puppy out of the car, and have a wild game of fetch or some other game he enjoys.

Remember to never leave your puppy in a vehicle. Even if the temperature is cool, it can heat up quickly inside your vehicle when the sun is shining, even with windows cracked.

Teaching "On" and "Off"

Instead of having to push your puppy off the couch all the time, it is far easier to teach your puppy cues to tell him when it is okay to be up on the furniture and when it is time to get off. Obviously, you can't teach him to get off something unless he is already on it, so it helps to teach these cues together.

You will need your puppy, clicker, treats, and something easy for him to jump up onto. In this example we are using a suitcase. Before you start, make sure the puppy is not afraid of the object you want him to jump on. If he is, try something else.

Use hand targeting to get the puppy to come near the object he will jump onto. Click and treat him for touching the target near the suitcase.

Position your target hand so the puppy would have to reach up slightly above the top of the suitcase. Click and treat each target.

Move your target hand back so the puppy has to reach to touch the hand. You want him to put his front feet on the suitcase in order to reach the hand. Continue to click and treat for him to touch your target hand.

Continue moving your target hand back so the puppy has to move more of his body onto the suitcase in order to touch the hand. Click and treat each target.

Once your puppy has all four feet on the suitcase, have a big party with lots of praise and treats and ask him to get off the suitcase by either having him target your hand off (which you click and treat) or show him a treat and toss it off the suitcase.

When the puppy is jumping onto the suitcase every time you present your hand target over it, give this a cue such as "on." When he is jumping off the suitcase every time you present your hand target off the suitcase, give it the cue "off."

Once you think your puppy understands "on" and "off," reward him only for jumping up when you ask or jumping off when you ask. If he jumps up on the suitcase without your cue, don't reward him—walk away instead. Once you have mastered on and off the object you were using, practice with other objects the puppy can get on.

Teaching "Sit"

Sit is a behavior most puppies do naturally. Because humans get excited when the puppy sits, the puppy quickly learns the action increases the possibility of praise or treats. If your puppy does not offer a natural sit behavior, you can teach him via either targeting or luring to go into the sit position. You will need your puppy on a leash in a distraction-free area with plenty of treats as well as your clicker.

Using your target hand, ask the puppy to touch your hand just above his nose. You want him turning his head slightly up, but not too high. Click and treat him for targeting his nose up.

Position your target hand so the puppy has to reach up slightly higher and click and treat this behavior.

Continue to position your target hand so he has to move his head up and back more and more. Click and treat whenever he touches your hand. Go slow and don't ask the puppy to reach higher than he is comfortable.

If you want to lure your puppy into a sit, place a treat in your hand and put it right above his nose. Move your hand up and back and he will follow the treat until his butt is on the floor. Use the steps below and reward the puppy by releasing the treat to him at first when he just has his nose up and back a little bit, and then asking for more of the behavior before you release the treat. Use the food lure only a few times. After that, use your hand without food in the exact same way. The puppy will think the food is in your hand and follow it so he is in the sitting position. Give him lots of treats and praise after he is sitting.

At some point you will have moved your target hand up and back enough that the puppy will have to squat in order to touch your hand. Eventually this will lead to a sit with his butt all the way on the floor. The first time he gets into a full sit, give him many treats and lots of praise. Once he is sitting 80 percent of the time when you position your hand above his head, begin to use the "sit" cue.

Fade the use of your hand above the puppy's head and just use the word "sit." To fade the hand signal, gradually make your hand less of a target. If he gets stuck and suddenly can't figure out what he is doing, go back to using your hand target more, then try fading when the pup is more confident.

Once you are sure your pup understands "sit," do not reward him for sitting unless you have asked him to do so. Never repeat the cue. If the puppy does not sit when you ask him to, take a step and ask him again. If he will not sit on cue after you have tried this three to five times, go back to hand targeting the sit, as he just doesn't get the concept of the word yet.

Teaching "Down"

Down can be confusing for some dogs because people tend to use the word to also mean get off of a person or to get off the furniture. If you teach your dog to lie down, give it a cue that you don't also use to mean get off of something. So if you teach your dog the cue "down" to mean lie down, don't say "down" to ask him to get off the couch or to stop jumping on people. Teach other cues for those behaviors.

Don't start on "down" until you have a very good "sit" first. Wait to teach this behavior until you no longer need to click and treat every time the dog sits. To teach down, it is often helpful to be able to sit on the floor in front of your puppy. This can make some puppies super excited, so you may need to just practice sitting on the floor and teaching your puppy to sit first with you on the floor in front of him.

You will need your puppy, treats, and your clicker.

Ask the puppy to sit and tell him "good boy" rather than clicking and treating. Ask him to target your hand just below his nose. He doesn't have to target all the way to the floor. You just want him to look down and touch your hand. Click and treat. Place the treat on the ground rather than handing it to the puppy. You always want to place the treat where you want the puppy to eventually be.

Move your target hand closer to the ground and click and treat the puppy, again placing your treat on the ground between his paws. You want him to decide the floor is super interesting. Continue this step until your hand is all the way on the floor and your puppy is repeatedly targeting your hand. If he gets up from his sit, ask him to sit again. You want the puppy to be sitting at the beginning while you are targeting the down.

Move your hand on the floor so the puppy now has to stretch his neck to target. You want to get him to stretch out without getting up from the sit. Soon the puppy will stretch a paw out. Click and treat any movement that is causing him to move his front legs out.

Repeat step 3 until the puppy stretches his front legs out enough that he lies down. At this point, give him huge amounts of praise and a handful of treats between his paws. Continue dropping treats between his paws if he stays down.

Toss a treat a few feet away so your puppy has to go get it Then have him come back, ask him to sit, and repeat these steps until he is lying down as soon as he starts to follow the hand target. Once he is reliably lying down 80 percent of the time, give it a cue such as "down" and then start practicing it in a new location.

An Easier Method for Teaching the Down

For some puppies, it is easier to get them to down using your leg or a chair. You need something that the puppy can get under, but once under it, he can't stand all the way up. What you use will depend on how tall your puppy is. You also need something he is not scared of. For this we will use a leg, but the steps would be the same no matter what you use.

You will need your puppy, a comfortable place to sit on the floor, treats, and your clicker.

Extend your leg and raise it off the floor just enough for the puppy to crawl under it. Place the puppy so he has to be on one side of your leg, but to target he would have to reach under your leg to touch your hand. Click and treat him for touching your hand, and place the treat so he has to stick his head under your leg to get it. Always put the treat on the floor.

Target the puppy so he has to put more of his body under your leg. Click and treat and continue to place the treat so the puppy has to move more of his body under the leg to get it.

Once the puppy has about half of his body under your leg, feed him a few treats in that position. If he can't quite stand up, chances are very good he will lie down. Click and treat with lots of praise.

Repeat these steps until the puppy lies down immediately after targeting under your leg. At this point give it the cue "down" and begin to take your leg out of the equation. You can raise your leg up more and just use it as a guide. Most puppies learn to watch your hand that was providing the treat, so that hand also can become a down cue to use to ask the puppy to "down" once you are no longer using your leg as a guide.

Teaching "Stay" and "Come"

Stay and come are easy to teach together. Do not teach "stay" and "come" until after you have already taught your puppy a stationary behavior such as "sit" or "down." You will need your puppy on a leash, your treat bag, clicker, and a distraction-free area.

Stand right in front of your puppy and ask him to sit. Wait one or two seconds, then ask him to come as you take a step backward. If you have been using your hand to target your puppy, have him target your hand as you say "come." You will immediately reward him with a high-value treat if he comes to you, or click and treat if he targets your hand.

Reward the puppy with the treat in your hand and your hand resting on your leg. You want the puppy to be as close to you as possible when you are working on "come." If you reward him when he is a few feet away from you, it will make catching him more difficult once you take this behavior off leash.

You will gradually wait longer and longer before asking your puppy to "come." In this way the puppy learns to sit until you ask him to come to you. You can add the cue "stay" after you ask the puppy to sit.

Do not make your puppy wait a few seconds longer each time before you ask him to come. If you do, he may realize this is a game he can never win, as no matter how well he does, you will make him sit longer the next time. You want to gradually increase the time you ask him to sit, but occasionally release him more quickly so he can't predict what you will want.

If your puppy moves before you ask him to come, don't say anything. Just place him back in the spot where he was before he moved and ask him to "come" faster for a few repetitions.

Slowly work up to getting your puppy to sit and stay for 30 seconds before going on to the next step. Stay can be super boring for puppies, so break training into short sessions punctuated by a lot of play.

Once the puppy can sit for 30 seconds, begin to move farther away from him. The first time you move back more than a step, ask the puppy to come after just one or two seconds. Your moving will probably excite him, and you need him to be able to win this new version of the game.

As the puppy learns to sit and stay while you move farther away from him, you will gradually increase the time he can sit back up to 30 seconds until you are able to be at the end of a 6-foot (1.82m) leash and your puppy can sit there for at least 30 seconds. Once you have this mastered, you can just begin asking the puppy to sit for longer and longer sessions before you call him to you.

Stay and Come Games

You can play games with your puppy that involve him coming to you when he is not also doing a sit/stay. You will need your puppy and two people, each with a clicker and treats. This game works best if you can start it in a hallway or other place where the puppy will have very few options where he can go.

1. The people should stand a few feet apart with the puppy in the middle. Ask the puppy to target your hand, then click and treat when he does. Hold the treat in your hand with your hand resting on your leg so the puppy will learn to come as close to you as possible.

2. The second person should immediately ask the puppy to target her hand. Click and treat when the puppy does so, again with the reward resting on the person's leg.

3. Once the puppy is easily going back and forth, each person should take one step backward so you increase the distance between you. If the puppy is coming and targeting each person's hand, introduce your cue such as "come" or "here." Continue to gradually increase the distance between the people.

4. When the puppy is reliably running back and forth between each person at a distance of about 10 feet (3m), change the game so he has to target your hand and then sit before you click and treat. Cue the word "sit" as soon as the puppy touches your hand. Keep the treat close to your body so he is as close to you as possible when you ask him to come. Soon he will automatically sit each time you ask him to come.

5. Continue to practice until the puppy is always sitting when he comes to you. Next ask the puppy to come to you, and as soon as he sits, put your hand on his collar and say something like "gotcha." Click and treat only after the puppy has come to you, sat, and you have grabbed his collar. This way the puppy will learn that coming to you requires him to sit and wait until you have touched his collar. This is important because if your puppy were really loose, you would want him to understand "come" means come and sit still until you can grab his collar.

6. Keep increasing the distance and then take your recall to a different room and eventually outside. Do not let your puppy off leash until your recall is 100 percent perfect while he is on leash. Practice distance with the puppy on a 20- or 30-foot (6 to 9m) long leash.

Teaching "Leave It"

One of the best things you can teach your puppy is to leave something alone. It could be a piece of food dropped on the floor or your pizza sitting on the coffee table.

Start in a distraction-free area with your puppy on a leash. Have your clicker and a bag of high-value treats. You will also need something edible but hopefully not as desirable as the high-value treats. Generally, it works if you start with a dry dog biscuit as your boring item.

Show the puppy the dry dog biscuit and put it under your foot. You will need to wear heavy shoes that completely cover your feet. Wait quietly for the puppy to stop trying to get the biscuit. The second he backs off from your shoe, click and toss him a high-value treat.

Repeat step 1 until the puppy stops trying to get the dog biscuit as soon as he sees you put it under your shoe.

Leave the dog biscuit uncovered, but near your shoe. If the puppy looks at the biscuit but then looks back at you, click and treat. If he tries to get the biscuit, cover it with your shoe and wait for him to stop before you click and treat.

Pick up the biscuit and move it to a new location and repeat steps 1 through 3 until your puppy begins to understand that no matter where you put this biscuit he can't have it, but if he leaves it alone you will give him something better. As he looks at the biscuit, give the cue "leave it."

Next, leave the biscuit uncovered for longer and with your foot farther away. As the puppy approaches the biscuit say "leave it" and if he does, click and treat. If he just continues to stare at the biscuit but doesn't try to eat it, wait for him to look at you and then click and treat. If he tries to get the biscuit, cover it with your foot.

After the puppy understands "leave it" with your biscuit on the floor, move the biscuit to the edge of something raised and repeat the steps, this time using your hand to cover the biscuit. First you will just cover the biscuit and wait for the puppy to back off, then click and treat. Follow the same steps as above.

Begin using a higher-value treat such as a moist dog treat rather than the dry biscuit, and start over from step 1.

Once your puppy understands the Leave It game, you can take objects such as your shoe, pieces of trash, or anything you want your puppy to leave alone and teach him using the same steps. Leave it is only for objects the puppy has not picked up yet. If the puppy has something in his mouth you don't want him to have, teach "Drop It," which is covered in Chapter 12.

Choosing a Trainer and Training Class

While you can teach many behaviors on your own, taking your puppy to a training class is extremely important. Many puppy classes allow off-leash play, which is necessary for puppies to learn how to interact with other dogs. Puppies biting other puppies often learn that biting too hard makes play stop, which is important when you want them to learn to stop biting *you*.

It is also important to go to a class so your puppy can learn to work around distractions. It is one thing to learn "sit" while he is in your living room, and quite another to learn to sit with several other puppies around. A trainer can also help you refine your technique and come up with solutions to problems. While this book gives you common examples of how to train various behaviors, dog training is not a "one-size-fits-all" concept. What works for one puppy may not work as well for another.

What to Look For

The key to choosing a trainer and training class is to find a place where you feel comfortable with the person teaching the class and the techniques used to teach the puppies.

First, find trainers who specialize in positive training techniques. If you go to a trainer who wants to put a choke chain or a prong collar on your puppy, keep looking. Once you identify trainers who teach in a positive manner, look at types of classes offered, times of classes, what the puppies will learn, etc. Do not pick a trainer based solely on price. While you want the best deal possible, cheaper is not always better.

The next step is to see if the trainer offers a free orientation to let you know more about his or her classes or if it is possible to sit in on a class (without your puppy) and observe how the class is run. If you observe a class and see the clients having fun with their puppies and interacting well with the trainer, chances are you will also enjoy the class.

The trainer you choose needs to be good not only at working with puppies, but also at dealing with people. Many people are great at training the dog, but are unable to adequately communicate with the human holding the leash. Choose a trainer who speaks to you in easy-to-understand language versus training jargon. You also want a trainer who can break down what you are learning into easy-to-follow steps.

Find out if your entire family can attend the training, as it is very important for all family members to be on board with whatever you are working on with the puppy. If you have children who are old enough to sit quietly and not disrupt a class, see if it is okay if they attend the class as well.

Private Training and Board-and-Train Options

While group training classes can be great for puppy socialization and to work on distractions, many trainers also offer private training. This might be beneficial if you are having a very specific issue or an issue tied directly to your home or to certain family members. For example, if your puppy is great with everyone in the family except the 6-year-old, having a private session to work with just the puppy and the 6-year-old would be appropriate.

Some trainers offer board and train options, which can seem very attractive. You drop your puppy off for a day (or a week) and come back to a trained dog. Board and train works best if you drop your puppy off each day and then spend time at the end of the day working with the trainer on what your puppy learned. If you choose to do board and train, inspect the facility where your puppy will be staying and see how the puppies are treated, both during training and when they are not being formally trained. Remember, your puppy is always learning and you don't want him to be in a stressful environment.

Chapter 11

Solving Problem Behaviors

- Stop your puppy from barking, biting, digging, and other unwanted behaviors.
- Fix lingering housetraining issues.

We often inadvertently teach a puppy the very behaviors we don't like, such as jumping up, barking, biting, and running off with a shoe. Your puppy wants your attention, so if he jumps up on you and you yell at him or push him off, he just got what he wanted. If you are watching television and ignoring him, he might come over and grab your arm because in the past that made you interact with him. It doesn't matter to the puppy that you are not happy with the interaction; he just wanted your attention.

Many puppies quickly learn how to get you to play games of run, chase, and tug. If your puppy takes your shoe and you chase him and try to get the shoe back by pulling on it, you just played run, chase, and tug. If a puppy grabs the pant leg of a 6-year-old, the child generally starts hopping and screaming, causing the puppy to think he just created the best squeaky toy ever.

The best training is to ignore behavior you don't want and reward behavior you do want. You can also think about training an incompatible behavior. Jumping up is a good example. You can ignore your puppy jumping on you, thus preventing the dog from getting the attention he seeks. Or you can teach him to "sit," because if he is sitting, he cannot possibly jump up on you.

It is important to not let problem behaviors get out of hand. Often owners wait until a behavior has become chronic and they just can't stand it anymore. Fixing problem behaviors takes time. It is far easier to fix an issue as soon as it starts than to wait for it to go away. When problem behaviors involve children, especially nipping or biting, consult a professional trainer as soon as possible.

Jumping Up on People

Puppies love to jump up on their humans. When puppies are small, people often talk to them or pet them when they jump up, which rewards the puppy for the behavior. Then when the puppy gets bigger, the owner decides the behavior isn't so cute and tries to stop it. This can be very confusing for a puppy who has been rewarded for jumping up for months.

If you don't ever want your puppy to jump up on a person, do not reward this behavior from the beginning. This is one of the most difficult behaviors for people to fix, because no matter how careful you are, someone in the family, or a family friend, or a complete stranger on a walk will bend over and pet the puppy as she jumps up, or talk to her when she is jumping up.

Jumping up can also be an attention-seeking behavior, so even if you are saying words like "no" or "off" or pushing your puppy away from you, you still are giving her attention. You need to ignore this behavior and reward the puppy only if she approaches you and keeps four feet on the floor. Everyone who encounters her has to be told to ignore the jumping-up behavior.

If your puppy jumps up on a person, ask that person to stand still with her arms folded and her head and eyes turned away from the puppy. This takes away the person's attention. If the puppy gets down, ask the person to take a step closer, and if the puppy remains with four feet on the floor, praise her and throw her a treat. Some people reward their puppy the second she gets off of a person, but this could teach her the best way to get a treat is to jump up and then immediately get off. You need to reward only the correct behavior and ignore anything else.

To begin teaching this you will need treats, two people, and your puppy on a leash.

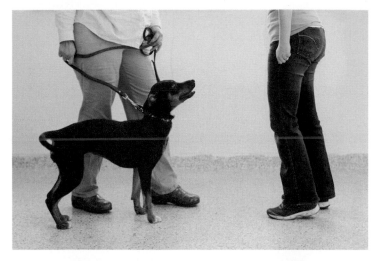

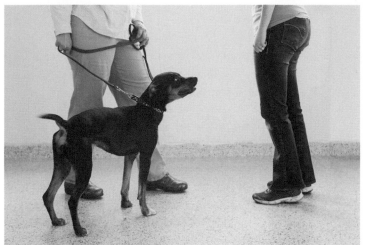

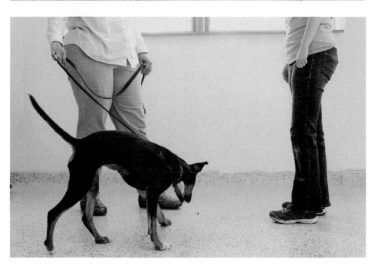

1. One person holds the puppy's leash, while the other person approaches the puppy. If the puppy jumps up on the person approaching, that person should turn and walk away. Repeat this until the puppy isn't jumping up when the person approaches. The person approaching should click and treat when the puppy has four feet on the floor as he or she approaches.

2. If the puppy repeatedly jumps up when a person approaches, have the person approaching the puppy toss a treat from farther away. Wait for a time when the puppy's feet are on the floor, and click and treat. Soon the puppy will learn it is her four feet on the floor that is winning the reward and the person can begin coming closer.

3. Once the puppy understands that the reward comes from not jumping up, the person approaching should begin to toss the treat toward the person holding the leash. You want the treat to land near the shoe of the person holding the leash. Soon the puppy will realize that when a person approaches, food will appear near the person holding the leash, and she will begin staying by her owner's side when another person approaches.

Once the puppy has mastered this part of the game, the person holding the leash will begin rewarding the puppy rather than the person approaching doing it.

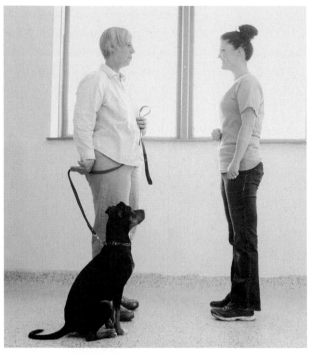

1. Hold the leash and ask the other person to walk toward you. Click and treat the puppy for remaining at your side. If she rushes forward to jump on the person, have the person walk away. Soon the puppy will learn that she is getting the reward for staying by your side while a person approaches and that her reward goes away if she jumps up on the person.

2. The next step is to act more like a real-life situation. On a walk people are not going to turn around and walk away if your puppy jumps on them. You want to teach the puppy that having people speaking to her or petting her still requires her to not jump up.

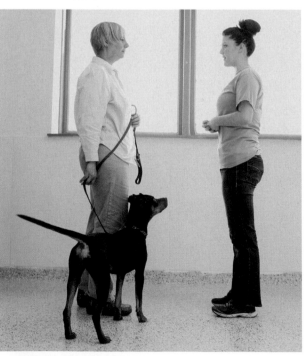

3. Ask another person to approach and talk to the puppy in a normal tone. In the beginning, ask the person to avoid eye contact and avoid petting the puppy. You just want the puppy to keep four feet on the floor while someone else is talking.

4. Next you will have the person approaching act more excited, speaking in a high-pitched voice that people often use when they see babies or puppies. Again you will reward the puppy for keeping her feet on the floor, and if she jumps up the treats and the person go away.

5. Once the puppy has mastered keeping her feet on the floor while someone is talking, begin allowing the person approaching to pet the puppy. In the beginning, reward the puppy heavily for keeping her feet on the floor while the person is petting her. Later, being petted will be a reward in itself.

You need to play this game with 20 or more people of all different ages, shapes, and sizes for the puppy to begin to understand it works with everyone.

Another option is to teach your puppy the word "sit" and ask her to sit every time a person approaches. If she is sitting, she cannot possibly jump up. You would use the same techniques, but ask the puppy to sit when the person approaches. If she stands up, the person approaching moves away.

Barking

You will never completely stop your puppy from barking, nor should you want to. You want him to let you know if he needs to go out to potty or if something is amiss in the house.

First determine why your puppy is barking. Puppies quickly learn that if they bark at you, you do something fun such as talk to them (even yelling "shut up" is talking to them), or you feed them or give them a treat to try to distract them. In all of these examples, you are actually teaching the puppy that barking gets rewards. So for attention-seeking barking, ignore it completely. Soon the puppy will learn barking gets her nothing and she will stop.

Dogs bark out the window at people going by because from the dog's perspective, he barks and the people go away. If you want to train your dog to not bark out the window, you have to ensure he is not doing this when you are not home. You could crate him, block access to rooms that look out on a street, close the curtains, or invest in window film that obscures the view.

When you are home, stay with your dog, and if he barks give him a cue such as "thanks." If he looks at you when you say "thanks," click and treat. You may need to start with him on a leash far from the window. If he is too intent on barking, he won't hear you speaking to him. Soon he will realize the word "thanks" is followed by a reward. By gradually increasing the distance you are from the dog when you say "thanks," you could get to the point where you are in another room, you hear the dog bark, you say "thanks," and he runs to you for a treat.

You can also put barking on cue so that you can teach the cue "quiet" as well. You can't teach the "quiet" cue unless the dog has learned to "speak" on cue.

You will need your puppy on a leash, your clicker and treats, and a way to make the puppy bark. If your puppy barks when someone knocks on the door, start with that.

1. Knock on the door. If the puppy barks, click and treat. Repeat this step four or five times.

2. Wait for a few seconds and see if the puppy barks without you knocking on the door. If so, click and treat that; if not, go back to Step 1.

3. Once the puppy is barking without the knock, give it a cue such as "speak" right as you think she is about to bark, then click and treat.

4. Begin to give the "speak" cue earlier, and click and treat if she barks on cue. Once the puppy knows the word "speak," reward her only when she speaks on cue. If she barks and you didn't ask her, have her perform another task, such as "sit." Reward that, then use "speak," and if she barks on cue reward her.

5. When she is barking on cue, say the word "quiet" and give her a treat (even if she is barking). Repeat this and she will anticipate the treat when she hears the word "quiet," and often will stop barking so she can eat the treat. If she stops barking on the word "quiet," click and treat.

Begging

Oh, those puppy eyes and that face are hard to resist. The puppy looks at you and you melt and give him affection or a treat. Remembering that he is always learning, you just taught him that if he looks at you just right, you will give him a reward. Begging doesn't just mean a problem at mealtime; it can happen anytime you are doing something else, the puppy comes up to you begging for attention, and you give in to his sweet face.

If you have children, especially young children who drop food, it is best to keep the puppy crated during mealtimes. Otherwise he will quickly learn to camp out near a child's chair. He may then decide jumping up on children is a faster way to get food.

Children who carry food and eat as they walk are a huge temptation to puppies. Depending on the age of the children, it may be better to crate the puppy during snack time rather than ask the children to make sure they are not feeding the puppy snacks or dropping them as they walk. Puppies often learn to follow children and then grab at their hands for food.

In an adult-only household, it is up to you whether you want to give the puppy food from your plate. So many people admit to giving their dog human food that it is important to at least have the discussion. If you are the type of person who just can't resist, set rules. If the puppy is in your face, whining, or pawing, don't give him food. If he is standing a short distance from you being polite, whether to reward him with food from your plate is up to you (as long as it's a safe food for him).

If you want your puppy to never have human food and you never want her being underfoot while you are eating, never feed her food from your plate. When you are having a meal, give her something to do. Put her on a mat or blanket with a long-lasting chew or food-dispensing toy.

Another issue is toys. When your puppy is small and it toddles up to you with a toy in her mouth, it is super cute. Most people give in, get the toy, and play with the puppy. Fast forward a few months and ask yourself how cute a 70-pound German Shepherd is going to be constantly dropping a toy in your lap while you are trying to watch television.

It is far easier to set rules in the beginning. If your puppy brings you a toy, ignore her for a few minutes and then go get another toy and play. Or initiate play first rather than waiting for the puppy to bring a toy. In this way she will learn that bothering you will never start a game of fetch or tug. When you are done playing with her, give a very clear signal that play is over. You might say "all done" and give her a treat when you take the toy away for the last time. In this way she will know not to keep bugging you for one last toss of the ball.

Digging

Digging is natural, especially for terrier breeds and some hounds. A Dachshund might dig because he smells something like a mole or mouse and it's exciting to try to dig it up. Other dogs dig because they are bored.

The first step is to determine if the dog is digging up vermin or if he is just digging because there is nothing else to do. If he is digging up vermin, there isn't much you can do about that. The puppy is being a puppy and doing what his instincts tell him to do.

If the dog is bored, your job is to give him something to do. Many people think puppies will be happier being "free" outside. In reality, most puppies spend their time at the back door waiting for the human to come back out and interact with them. If the human doesn't come back out, the puppy is going to find something to do for entertainment. A simple solution is to not leave your puppy alone for long periods of time in your backyard. If you cannot keep your puppy inside for some reason, build an outdoor kennel so you have someplace safe to keep him when you can't be in the yard playing with him.

There are lots of things you can do to make your yard more entertaining.

Make your puppy his own digging pit. Get play yard sand and dig a hole 8 to 12 inches (20 to 30.5cm) deep and several feet wide. At first put treats on top of the sand, then begin burying the treats just under the sand. Work up to burying treats and toys farther down. Soon the puppy will run to his sand pile and happily dig there rather than in your yard.

Teach your puppy to hunt. Show him a handful of treats and toss them in the grass right in front of his nose. Begin throwing the treats farther from the puppy's nose. Give him a cue such as "find." As the puppy gets better at finding, scatter your yard with treats while he is inside and then ask him to hunt for them. Your puppy will soon learn to spend time exploring the yard for the treats with his nose.

Make your pup a frozen hanging treat. Get a small bucket and fill it with water and perhaps a bit of chicken or beef broth. Place a long chain in the bucket and put in bits of dry kibble, treats, and, depending on your dog, maybe a ball. Freeze this mixture. Once it is frozen, remove the bucket and hang the frozen treat from a stake or post in the yard. You want it just a little off the ground so the puppy has to jump at it to interact. As it melts, fun things will fall out.

Chewing

Like digging, chewing is something puppies do naturally. They are honing their jaw strength, learning to hunt, and, depending on their age, they may be chewing because they are teething. You cannot stop the puppy from chewing. Instead, you have to channel the chewing into something appropriate.

A common complaint from puppy owners is that the puppy has "lots" of toys, but still prefers to chew on shoes, people, chair legs, etc. Find out what the puppy seems to want to chew on the most in your house and then try to find things that mimic that item. Toys may not always be the best chew options. You want to find something your puppy will lie down with and chew on. This will provide him with a lot of fun chewing satisfaction, and is a good way to keep him out of your way for a bit.

Talk to other puppy owners and find out what keeps their puppy busy. Common items that seem to work for many puppies are raw bones, elk antlers, bully sticks, or hollow rubber feeding toys filled with something good to eat. Talk to your veterinarian about chewing options. Some vets do not recommend rawhide products. Others might not recommend raw bones.

If your puppy is chewing on something you don't want him to have, avoid making a huge game out of taking it away. Puppies often learn to take your shoe because you will chase them and then play tug to get it back. It is far better to quietly trade for something more appropriate. Obviously, if the puppy has something potentially dangerous, do whatever you can to get it away from him as quickly as possible.

For heavy chewers it is a good idea to feed them out of rubber feeding toys. These are hollow, generally egg-shaped toys designed to hold food or treats.

Measure your puppy's dry kibble for an entire day into a mixing bowl. Add a little water and some truly tasty tidbit such as peanut butter or spray cheese.	Mix this up and divide it among a number of hollow rubber feeding toys. Put a bit of the peanut butter or cheese in the hole on the end of the toy to act as a cap to keep the food mixture inside.	Give one of the feeding tubes to the puppy and see how he reacts to it. If he loves it, freeze the tubes, which will make getting the food out a bit more difficult.

Every time you need to give your puppy something to chew on, you can just feed him part of his daily ration of food. This helps keep puppies from getting fat from all the calories in things like bully sticks and other high-value food chews. If you use raw bones, you can also freeze them so that the puppy can chew on them longer. The trick is to find items the puppy will chew on for a long time.

If you have more than one dog, be careful when putting out high-value chew items. Many dogs do not share food or other valuable resources well. It may be a good idea to separate dogs and puppies when giving out high-value items.

Nipping and Biting

A huge frustration for many owners is how much puppies nip and bite. Puppy teeth are needle sharp, and they hurt. If your puppy is under 5 months, see if you can find a puppy class that allows puppies to play with each other. Puppies are very good at teaching each other how much bite pressure is too much.

It is also always good to find appropriate, friendly adult dogs for your puppy to play with. A good adult dog can also teach the puppy when biting is getting to be too much. It is impossible for people to mimic what dogs do when biting hurts. However, some puppies will respond to a high-pitched "yelp" from a person. If your puppy bites you, try yelping and see if he stops and backs off. If he becomes more excited and bites you harder, don't repeat that exercise. Some puppies are very good at responding to a human yelp, while others find it highly exciting.

Whenever possible, ignore nipping and biting. You may need to wear heavier clothing until you can teach the puppy you don't enjoy that attention. If you scream, jump around, yell, or push the puppy when he nips you, he will just decide he has invented the most fun game ever. One good trick is to stand completely still with your arms folded and turn your head away from him. Many puppies will read this as a cutoff signal and back away from you. If you aren't fun when the puppy bites you, he will generally stop playing that game.

If the puppy is biting your legs as you walk through the house, put a toy on a rope and drag the toy after you. This is especially helpful for children who are being bitten. The puppy will learn to go after the toy rather than the human legs.

Also make sure your puppy has plenty of fun things to chew on. If you can put something in his mouth that he can chew on, he is less likely to try nipping you.

Unfortunately, there are going to be times when your puppy turns into a little monster who just can't be deterred from biting. Like babies, puppies can become overstimulated, especially near nap time, and nothing you can do will calm them down. At this point you need to put your puppy in his crate or in his room. You don't want to make it a punishment, so don't drag the puppy to his crate. Ask him to go into his crate and give him something to chew on. Leave him there for half an hour or so and let him come back out when he is calm. You can also walk away from him and put a door between you and the puppy teeth. He should learn that when he bites too much, you go away from him.

Never start out teaching your puppy biting games. Many people think it is fun to grab the puppy's muzzle or let him bite them when he is little. This is just going to turn your puppy into a dog who thinks grabbing your arm or hand is okay.

Nipping and biting are much harder to manage when young children are involved, because kids make great squeaky toys. The puppy bites, the child runs and screams, and the puppy is rewarded by a fun game of chase. Read the section on games for children in Chapter 12 for help with children and nipping.

If you can't stop your puppy nipping and biting, you need to consult a professional trainer or behaviorist. The longer the behavior continues, the harder it will be to correct.

Leash Issues

Pulling while walking on a leash is one of the most common issues for puppy parents. Even if you are using a no-pull harness, chances are you will still need to help your puppy learn not to pull.

Do not use a retractable leash, as these just teach the puppy to pull harder because every time he pulls, he gets more leash.

Stop and Go can be a very effective way to teach puppies not to pull. You don't need food or a clicker for this exercise. Going for the walk is the reward.

Keep the hand holding the end of the leash tucked to your stomach. No matter how hard your puppy pulls, you cannot extend your arm. The puppy needs to always know how much leash he has to work with, and he needs to learn that pulling will not result in more leash.

If your puppy pulls, stop. Do not move. Do not talk to him or jerk on the leash. Just stand still and ignore him.

At some point the puppy will take a step back and provide you with slack in the leash or he will turn and look at you. The second this happens, praise him and move forward again.

When the puppy pulls, stop again and wait for slack or for him to turn back to you, then praise him and move forward.

It may take you a while to go for a very long walk when you first begin using Stop and Go, but once the puppy figures out he can't move forward whenever he feels pressure on his neck, he will learn to walk so there is no pressure on his neck. Thus he won't be pulling your arm. In order for Stop and Go to work, everyone in the family has to do the same thing and you have to do it for the entire walk. If one person uses Stop and Go and another allows the puppy to pull as hard as he wants, he will not learn to walk on a loose leash.

In addition to Stop and Go, teach your puppy that sometimes you may make unexpected direction changes. This will keep him on his toes and teach him to pay attention to where you are and what you are doing.

1. If your puppy is far ahead of you, call his name and suddenly do a U-turn and walk the other way. You don't want to startle him or jerk his neck, which is why you want to call his name first. You should give this change in direction a cue such as "let's go."
2. When the puppy is far ahead of you again and not paying attention, call his name, say your cue, and do a U-turn. Soon he will figure out that you are not predictable and he needs to pay attention.

Using Stop and Go and the U-turn together can be very effective in teaching the puppy to walk on a loose leash. If your puppy is not pulling, praise him. You need to provide lots of positive feedback whenever he is not pulling too hard.

If your issue is a puppy who bites his leash constantly while you walk, put a toy on a rope and drag that with you. The puppy will then have something he can grab onto in his mouth. Do not play tug games if he has the leash in his mouth. Remember, tug is fun. If the puppy grabs the leash and you tug to get it back, he will continue to want to play this game. Instead, hold on to your puppy's collar and drop the leash. At some point he will let go. Praise the puppy, pick up the leash, and walk. Continue to do this until he realizes that tugging on the leash means the walk just stops and no tugging is happening.

Another common leash problem is a puppy who lies down and won't move. If that happens, ask your puppy to target your hand. Once he targets, click and treat and throw the treat a few inches forward. It is better to try to keep your puppy moving before he lies down, so if you see him start to lag behind, ask him to target and throw the treat ahead of him.

If your puppy does lie down, do not pull or drag him. This will frighten the puppy and generally cause him to pull back even more. Instead, stop, give him plenty of slack in the leash, and squat down. See if you can call the puppy to you. If he is frightened by something on the walk, do whatever you can to increase the distance between the scary object and the puppy. Give him lots of treats for looking at the scary object. You want him to always think walks are fun. Also avoid picking your puppy up whenever he won't move. At some point your pup may be too big to pick up. If he is a small dog, you still want him to learn to walk on his own and not depend on you to pick him up whenever he no longer wants to move.

Incomplete Housetraining

Peeing and pooping in the house is one of the top reasons dogs are surrendered to shelters or rehomed. For a refresher on housetraining, refer to Chapter 6.

There are many reasons dogs continue to pee or poop in the house, but the top two are stress and never really understanding they are to go outside. However, if you have a puppy that was perfectly housetrained and suddenly begins to have accidents, consult a veterinarian immediately. Parasites or urinary tract infections can cause puppies to suddenly start eliminating in inappropriate places.

Not Properly Trained as a Puppy

Most adult dogs that aren't fully housetrained were just never completely trained as puppies. You have to be consistent in housetraining and reward the puppy for going outside (or if you are training to an indoor spot, reward him for going there). Remember, the puppy has only a few seconds of association, so you have to go outside with him and give him the reward the second he is done peeing or pooping. If you can't watch him inside, he has to be crated until he is housebroken.

Getting Angry at the Puppy

Another cause of inappropriate elimination is getting angry at the puppy for peeing and pooping inside. This causes a great deal of stress and will actually increase the likelihood that the puppy will continue to potty in the house. Yelling can also provide attention so some puppies might pee in front of you just to get you to interact with them. It is often better to ignore the puppy completely, clean up the spot, and work to ensure he is getting out frequently.

Visiting Other Homes

Puppies that are housebroken in their own homes may not know what to do when they visit someone else's home. In the beginning, treat each new area as a place in which the puppy may pee or poop, and go back to crating and rewarding the puppy for eliminating in the appropriate new spots. If you teach your puppy a cue that means this is the place to potty, he will be likely to transition more easily to a new location.

If you take your puppy to a home in which there are other dogs, especially dogs that are not spayed or neutered, the chances are greater that the dogs will pee, especially on objects. Dogs mark territory so other dogs know they were there. If marking is an issue, try to keep the dogs away from the objects they are most likely to mark.

Stress

Moving, adding family members, traveling, illness of either the owner or the pet—all can also lead to housebreaking issues. If stress occurs, just be patient and go back to some basic housetraining. Chances are good that your puppy will quickly remember what he is supposed to do.

Resource Guarding

A *resource* is something the puppy decides he has to have. Some resources are obvious, such as food, water, and a place to sleep. Other resources might be toys, bones, or other valuable chewies. A resource could also be a person or a totally weird object, such as a piece of paper or a tissue. What a puppy considers a valuable resource may not make sense to us, but if it is something the puppy thinks is important, he may choose to keep a person or another dog away from it. This is called resource guarding.

Resource guarding kept dogs alive for centuries. Guarding the safest sleeping spots, the best food, and access to water from other dogs would have been key to survival. So in many ways, resource guarding is the correct answer from the puppy's perspective. Some puppies guard resources only from other dogs, while other puppies will also try to keep valuable resources away from a person they perceive is about to take it away. Many a person has been growled at or nipped taking a bone away from a puppy.

If you have multiple dogs that have serious fights over resources and you are unable to keep them separated, consult a professional trainer as soon as possible.

Resource Guarding at Mealtime

To start, if you have multiple dogs, get in the habit of feeding them in separate rooms or at least putting visual barriers between them while they are eating. Some dogs are fine eating near another dog, but others become very stressed. The dog doesn't know that food will always be available. He may worry that he has to eat his food fast to keep the other dog from getting it, or he may eat his food and then go to another dog's dish to eat that food as well. Even if all the dogs appear to tolerate this in the beginning, it can lead to problems down the road.

Dogs also don't have a sense of fairness. It doesn't matter to most dogs if all the other canines in the room have a bone. Some dogs will want all the bones. Until you know how your puppy reacts around valuable resources, do not leave him alone with other dogs when food or food-type items are on the floor. If one of your dogs is constantly stealing an item from another, separate the dogs whenever valuable resources are being given out. It is not fair to allow one dog to constantly bully another into giving up a coveted resource.

Never allow children to walk up to a dog that is eating or chewing on something. If children are too young to understand this, always separate them from the puppy when he is eating.

Teaching the Puppy to Let You Be Near When He Eats

If your puppy is guarding a resource from you, you can teach him that you actually have a better resource. We will use a puppy guarding a bowl of dry kibble in this example, but the steps would be similar with whatever is being guarded.

Find the distance you have to stand from your puppy while he is eating so that he isn't stressed by you being nearby. Watch his body language. If he stiffens, hunches down, eats faster, growls, or seems agitated, you are too close.

Once you find that distance at which your puppy doesn't care you are nearby while he is eating, toss hot dogs or other high-value treats toward his bowl. If you can get the hot dog into the bowl, that's even better.

Once the puppy realizes you are nearby and something even better than dry kibble is dropping into his bowl, take a tiny step closer and continue the game. You want to go slow and let the puppy know that your approach makes better things appear in the bowl. It may take many weeks before you can actually stand near the puppy while he is eating.

The puppy will eventually welcome your approach because you are making something better appear in his bowl and he will no longer be worried that you are going to take his resource away from him.

When You Are the Resource

If the puppy growls when a person or another pet approaches you, the puppy could be guarding you. After all, from the puppy's perspective you are very valuable and he may not wish to share you. If this happens, try ignoring the puppy and walking away. He may learn that guarding you has the opposite effect in that it makes you go away.

When it is the approach of another person toward you that triggers the guarding, have that person toss high-value treats to the dog as he or she approaches (using the same steps as for guarding kibble). In this way you teach the puppy that a person approaching makes better things happen.

Resource guarding is a serious issue, especially in homes with multiple pets or homes with young children. Don't hesitate to call a professional trainer as soon as possible for help with this behavior.

Chasing Things That Move

Fast-moving objects such as runners, bicycles, or vehicles often cause puppies to give chase.

Obviously, never letting your puppy loose in an area with moving vehicles is the first step to keeping him safe. Even if you live in the country, your puppy can be easily killed by a vehicle. Bicyclists and runners should not have to be terrorized by your dog, either, if they happen to be passing your home. Multiuse trails are extremely popular in cities and urban areas. Your puppy may be walking within mere feet of runners, bicyclists, and skateboarders. It is important to teach the puppy not to leap out or charge at these moving objects. In the following example we are going to use a puppy chasing a runner, but the steps would be the same for any moving object.

Have your puppy on a leash. You will need your clicker, treats, and some good friends who don't mind getting sweaty. Choose a location where you have plenty of room for a runner to go by you. Find the distance you need to be from the runner for the puppy to see the runner but not lunge or bark.

1. Click and treat the puppy for looking at the runner when he runs by. If the puppy is lunging and barking, you are too close to the runner.

2. After clicking and treating the puppy for looking at the runner when he passes five or six times, wait on the next pass from the runner and don't click the minute the puppy looks at him. Chances are good the puppy will look back at you when you don't click. Instantly click and treat that behavior. You want the puppy to look at the runner and then back at you.

3. Once you have the look-back behavior, give it a cue such as "look" or "watch me."

4. Slowly have the runner come closer to where you are standing with the puppy. Click and treat the puppy if he looks at the runner and looks back at you. If he loses focus and starts barking or lunging at the runner, move back. Keep your sessions short at first so the puppy can easily win.

5. Once the puppy looks at you when he sees a runner, start walking toward the runner rather than just standing in place while he runs by you. You may have to widen the distance between you and the runner when you add your own movement to the equation. Continue to click and treat the puppy for looking at you and not the runner.

Chapter 12

Having Fun with Your Puppy

- Games and tricks
- Play dates with other puppies
- An introduction to dog sports

Most people get a puppy to have fun with it, such as walking in the park or playing fetch. Many games people play with their puppy depend on its size and breed, and on the age of the person playing. Some people have an image of their puppy leaping through the air to catch a flying disc, but lots of dogs find an object sailing toward them scary. Whatever the game is, it has to be fun for both of you.

Some of the behavior issues people have with their dog begin because the dog is bored. Dogs are extremely intelligent. Many of them were originally bred to have a job, such as herding sheep. The traits that made them great at those jobs arc still there. There was also a time when dogs needed to hunt for their survival. Your dog is still a hunter.

Take those natural instincts and find ways to make games that use them to help your puppy grow up mentally and physically healthy. Hunting is a good example. If your puppy loves to run and pounce, put a furry toy on a rope and drag it along in front of her. Chances are she will think this is great fun. You just took the hunting instinct and made it into a game. Or you can take a handful of treats and throw them into the grass and let your puppy hunt for them.

If you want to do more, there are dozens of dog sports, and many are extremely welcoming of newcomers. Agility and competitive obedience are two activities that have multiple levels of participation. You can do them for fun, or you can set your sights on a world championship. If you have children, see if your local 4-H club offers a dog obedience program. It's great for the kids and the puppy.

Playing Tug

Tug is a game that's surrounded by controversy. You can find training books that say to never play tug with your dog, and websites that say you can play tug but you must always win the game. To add to the confusion, you can also find books that say some breeds have to win every time or they will stop playing.

In 2003, *The Journal of Applied Animal Welfare Science* published a report by Nicola J. Rooney and John W. S. Bradshaw of the Anthrozoology Institute at the University of Southampton. The study looked at play and its effect on the human and animal bond. The results of this study show evidence that playing tug and other interactive games can actually strengthen the relationship between owner and dog.

Tug is a great way to interact with your puppy. It's a game that many dogs enjoy, and it provides a nice aerobic workout for the dog. The trick to a successful game of tug is to have rules and to teach the puppy when to take the toy and when to give it back. Tug is a game best played between the puppy and older children or adults.

The first step is to find a toy your puppy enjoys tugging. Make sure it's long enough to allow you plenty of room to tug without getting too close to the puppy's mouth. Do not play tug with any toy that's completely in the puppy's mouth, such as a ball.

The first rule of tug is if the puppy's teeth ever touch your skin, even if it's an accident, the game is over. Drop the toy and walk away or give the puppy a treat to trade for the toy. Then pick up the toy and walk away. Don't get angry; just stop the game. Soon the puppy will learn to be careful where he puts his teeth.

The second rule is to always tell the puppy when the game is beginning and when it is over, versus allowing him to bring you a tug toy to initiate play. Tug is also the best way to teach your puppy the cue to let go of something. This is useful if he gets an item he shouldn't have, such as your shoe.

Do not play tug while your puppy is teething. If you pull on something that is in his mouth and his teeth hurt, he may decide tug is not a fun game.

Tug is all about movement. Think of your tug toy as a rabbit that's trying to evade a dog. The rabbit would make a lot of fast directional changes and would hop up and down. When you first begin playing tug, you may wish to have the puppy dragging a leash in case the game gets out of hand and you need to be able to control him.

For this game you will need a toy your puppy really enjoys chasing. It should be long enough to allow you plenty of room to keep your hands away from the puppy's mouth.

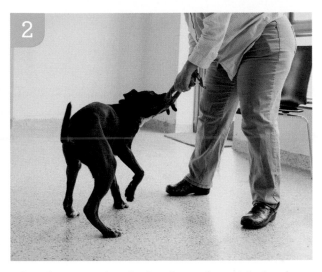

Show the puppy the toy, and start moving the toy around near him. When he takes the toy in his mouth, praise him and pull gently on the toy. If the puppy tugs back, immediately let go of the toy and let him run around with it for a few seconds.

After the puppy has had a victory lap with the toy, grab your end back and gently tug again. Let the puppy pull, then gently exert more pressure on your end so you are pulling the puppy toward you.

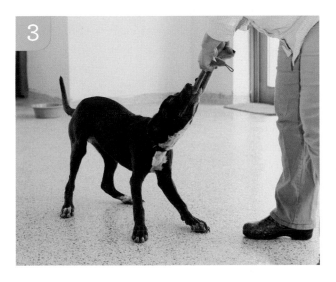

Go back and forth so sometimes the puppy is pulling the toy toward him and sometimes you are pulling the puppy toward you.

In the beginning, allow the puppy to win the toy often by gently letting go of the toy right when he is pulling back on it. Once the puppy thinks this is an awesome game, you can teach him the cue for "out." To avoid conflict until you teach the "out" cue, show the puppy a treat and then toss a few treats away from the toy so you can pick it up when he goes to get the treats.

1. Have the puppy on leash and get him tugging on the toy. Once he has the toy in his mouth, let go of it and put your hand through his collar or gently apply pressure to the leash to get him to stand still.

2. Because he's just standing there and you are no longer tugging the toy, it will become boring at some point and he'll open his mouth and drop it. The very second the puppy drops the toy, grab it and make it alive again as if the rabbit just jumped up to run away. The puppy will immediately want to pounce on it again. Play tug for a few minutes, then again let go of the toy and hold his collar until he drops the toy. Be sure to always let go of the toy completely so the puppy doesn't get any play action out of it.

3. Soon the puppy will understand that if he opens his mouth and drops the toy, the game of tug will immediately happen again. Once he's dropping the toy as soon as you touch his collar, give this the cue "out."

4. Next, begin to say the cue "out" without touching the puppy's collar. If he doesn't drop the toy, touch his collar until he does and keep working toward an "out" that doesn't need the collar prompt.

5. When you are done playing tug, give the puppy an "all done" cue as soon as you get the toy back, and give him a treat. Put the toy away so he can't see it.

Once you've taught an "out" cue with the tug toy, give the puppy other objects that you don't care if he has in his mouth. Gently tug, then ask for the out and immediately give him a treat when he drops the object. In this way you can get him to "out" no matter what object is in his mouth, including one of your best shoes.

If your puppy loves to play tug, use that to your advantage. Play a game of tug as a reward for obedience training. This will make the puppy look forward to training even more.

Teach the puppy to take the toy politely. When you ask him to sit, wait a few seconds and present the toy. If he jumps up to get it before you present it, take the toy away and ask for the sit again. Soon he will learn he has to sit politely until you ask him to take the toy.

Playing Fetch

It's best to first have an "out" cue before you start playing fetch with your puppy, so read teaching "out" in the tug section in this chapter before starting on fetch.

Some puppies will fetch naturally, meaning if you throw something they will run and pick it up. This type of puppy is generally very easy to teach fetch.

Let's use an example of a puppy who loves to chase tennis balls and pick them up. You will need two tennis balls and possibly a 20 or 30 foot (6 or 9m) long line.

1. Throw a ball and as soon as he picks it up, bounce a second ball. If the puppy runs back to you and drops the first ball, throw the second one.
2. If he runs back but doesn't drop the first tennis ball, use your "out" cue.
3. If that doesn't work, show the puppy a treat and as soon as he drops the ball, throw the second ball.

Soon the puppy will realize that bringing you the ball back and dropping it makes a second ball appear quickly. If he won't drop the ball or trade for a treat, avoid the temptation to try to pry it out of his mouth. That'll just make him want to hold on to it longer. Ignore him and walk away. He will learn that fetch isn't fun alone.

If your puppy fetches the ball but won't bring it back, put him on a 20 or 30 foot (6 or 9m) leash so you can control his movements. Walk up to him, ask him to out or trade him for a treat, and throw your second ball. If you taught your puppy to come to you on cue, ask him to come and then ask him to out the ball, and throw another ball immediately. The trick is to get the puppy to figure out that coming back to you and dropping the ball makes the next one appear quickly.

If your puppy doesn't naturally fetch, you can teach him. Just remember, some dogs are going to be more predisposed to want to play this game than others. If fetch turns out not to be your dog's favorite game, find something else to play with him.

To teach your puppy to fetch, you first have to teach him the cue "take it." Have your puppy on a leash, your clicker and high-value treats, and an object that he can easily put in his mouth. Start with something solid like a ball or a stick instead of a plush toy. For this demonstration we will use a tennis ball.

1. Hold the tennis ball right in front of the puppy's nose and click and treat for him to touch the ball with his nose. Get a few nose touches, take the ball away, and repeat until the puppy is reliably touching the ball with his nose every time you present it to him.

2. Hold the ball and don't click for just a nose touch; watch the puppy's mouth and if you see him open it (even slightly) click and treat that. If he licks the ball, you can also reward that behavior. The goal is to teach the puppy that you want more of his mouth open as it comes near the ball.

3. When the puppy is opening his mouth wide enough, place the ball in his mouth, click and treat (take the ball out of the mouth before you treat). If he does not like this step, go back to step 2 until he is putting his mouth over the ball on his own.

4. Once the puppy opens his mouth when he sees the ball, give this a cue such as "take it."

5. The next step is to teach the puppy to hold the ball for a longer period. Remember the click ends the behavior, so when you tell the puppy to take it, instead of immediately clicking and treating, you will wait a few seconds and then click and treat. If the puppy drops the ball before you have clicked, ask him to take it again and make the next repetition much shorter.

6. Teach the puppy to hold the ball until you ask him to "out."

Once the puppy understands "take it," you can put the ball on the floor and ask him to "take it." You may have to first just put your hand near the floor with the ball before the puppy understands he can pick up the ball off the floor. Once he can pick up the ball when you place it on the floor, you will toss the ball a few inches away and ask him to "take it." It's then just a matter of throwing the ball farther and farther and asking the puppy to "come" and "out" when he gets to you. You now have a game of fetch.

Playing Hide and Seek

Dogs love to use their noses to find things. What you ask your dog to find will depend on you. He could learn to find you and other family members, or treats or a favorite toy. If you want to be ambitious, teach your puppy to find a specific scent, put that scent on your remote control, hide it, and ask him to find it for you.

Whatever you want your puppy to find, the game will basically always work the same way. In this example we are going to use finding a person.

You will need two people and treats, and your puppy will need to be wearing a collar. Start the game standing near a doorway or someplace where it will be easy for a person to step just out of sight.

1. One person will hold the puppy by the collar and the person who will be hiding will stand right in front of the puppy and put the treats near the puppy's nose to tease him.

2. The person hiding will then take a step back and go behind the door. As soon as the person is out of sight, the person holding the puppy should let go of the collar.

3. If he runs to the person who is hiding, give him the treats and lavish praise. If the puppy won't follow the person, she should call the puppy.

4. You gradually make the game more difficult by asking the person hiding to move farther and farther away. Continue to tease the puppy with treats at first, but if he is readily running after the person, you can discontinue the teasing and simply have the person walk away.

5. If you are confident the puppy will run to the person when she's hiding nearby, give this a cue such as "seek." It's then just a matter of having the person hide in more and more difficult places.

If you want your puppy to find a favorite toy, you would tease him with the toy instead of food. Place the toy just out of sight and then praise the puppy when he finds the toy. Instead of calling that "seek," you could give it the cue for that specific toy, such as "bunny." That way you can amaze your friends by showing how your puppy can find specific toys when you give him the cue to "find your bunny." You would just teach him different words for different toys.

There are all kinds of things you can do if your puppy loves hide and seek. You could join a search and rescue team or look into the sport of K9 Nose Work. Nose Work is a sport sanctioned by the National Association of Canine Scent Work. You teach the dog to find specific scents and then take him to competitions where he'd have to find those scented objects.

Games to Play with Kids

How much interaction a child has with the puppy depends on the age of the child and the temperament of the puppy. For children under the age of 10 especially, always supervise play and ensure both the child and the puppy are having fun. If you see either child or puppy becoming tired or stressed, stop the activity.

Fetch and hide and seek are both awesome games children can play. Avoid rough-and-tumble games such as tug or run-and-chase games, especially for young children who may not know what to do if the puppy jumps on them or grabs an arm or leg.

Make sure children understand how to give the puppy a treat. The child should either drop the treat in front of the puppy or place it flat on her palm. Children should never offer the treat between their fingers, as that will teach the puppy to nip at the fingers.

Teach the child that if she wants the puppy to stop chasing her, she needs to stop and stand completely still, fold her arms, and stare at her feet. Puppies will generally not try to chase something that's not moving. You can increase the chance of success in this game by teaching the puppy it's fun to stop when the children stop.

Take your puppy to an area where the children can run and play, and have your clicker and treats with you.

1. Ask the children to run a few feet, then stop and "be a tree." The second the children stop, click and treat the puppy for being near the children with all his feet on the ground.

2. Continue playing this game and rewarding the puppy for not jumping up when the kids stop running.

3. Cue the puppy to sit when the children stop running, and click and treat. Repeat this many times. Soon the puppy will learn that when the children stop running and assume the "tree" position, he should sit.

Rope Circle

A fun game for a child old enough to use the clicker is to teach the puppy to run into a circle made with a rope. You can use the rope as a barrier to help contain your puppy, and it's a great game to teach kids clicker skills. You will need your puppy, a rope you can shape into a circle, the children, the clicker, and some treats. The circle should be big enough for the puppy to comfortably stand or lie down.

1. Toss a treat into the circle. When the puppy runs in and gets the treat, click and toss in another treat before he has a chance to get out of the circle. Have the children make a game of seeing how many clicks and treats they can give before the puppy comes out of the circle.

2. When the puppy comes out of the circle, have the children stay still near the edge of the rope and stare into the circle. If the puppy comes back to investigate, click and treat him for going back into the circle. Continue to click and treat him for staying inside the circle.

3. Once he understands being inside the circle is fun, have the children pick up the rope and move it and make a new circle. Click and treat the puppy for going back inside the circle.

4. When the puppy is reliably running into the rope circle whenever he sees it on the ground, ask him to do a "down" when he gets inside the circle. Continue this step until the puppy lies down whenever he goes into the rope circle.

5. Reward the puppy for being inside the rope circle for longer and longer periods of time. Always call him out of the circle so he learns to stay inside until he has the cue that he's done playing the circle game.

Hot and Cold

Hot and Cold is another awesome game children can play. You'll need your puppy, an object he can touch, a child, your clicker, and treats. For this example we use an orange plastic cone as the object we want the puppy to touch, but it could be just about anything.

1. Have the child stand near the orange cone and stare at it. If he is old enough to hold a leash and clicker and treats, allow him to be the operator. If necessary, the parent could hold the puppy on a leash, or could operate the clicker and let the child toss the treats.

2. The child should click and treat whenever the puppy looks at the cone. It's important that the humans all stare at the cone and not at the puppy. Even if you see the puppy just glance at the cone, click and treat.

3. Once the puppy figures out that looking at the cone is paying in treats, wait for him to reach out and sniff the cone. Then click and treat the puppy only if he sniffs the cone. If he gets distracted and stops sniffing the cone, go back to step 2 and just click and treat for looking a few times again.

4. Pick the cone up and move it to a new location, and click and treat the puppy for touching the cone with his nose.

5. When the puppy is reliably touching the cone every time you put it down, pick a new object and get him to touch that with his nose.

6. After the puppy has learned to explore different objects by touching them with his nose, put down two objects a short distance apart. Decide which one you want him to touch and then click and treat him for looking in the right direction, moving in that direction, and then finally touching the correct object. Remember, you're playing hot and cold. If the puppy looks at or interacts with the wrong object, just don't say anything. When he doesn't hear a click, he will realize that was the wrong answer.

Puppy Play Dates

While playing with the family is fun, playing with other dogs or puppies is a great way to entertain your puppy and provide some much-needed mental and physical exercise. If you have a puppy under 4 months of age, it's especially important to introduce him to as many well-trained puppies and adult dogs as you can find. The more puppies and dogs he can meet and have fun with when he's young, the more social he'll likely be as he grows up.

Finding Puppies to Socialize With

It's best to start puppy interactions under the guidance of a professional dog trainer, or with the help of someone at a doggy daycare who has the experience to know whether two puppies interacting are indeed having fun. If your puppy becomes scared of other dogs, you may spend your entire life dealing with a dog that's worried when he sees another dog out on a walk or in the park.

If you can't find a class that allows puppies to interact, ask friends, family, and co-workers to see if you can find puppies similar in age and size to yours. See the section in Chapter 3 on meeting other pets for tips on introducing your puppy to new dogs.

Is Your Puppy Having Fun?

Do not immediately step in if you hear growling or see fur stand up on the back of a dog or puppy. You may see some dogs show their teeth. You need the puppies to learn to communicate with the dogs they meet, so if you step in and stop every discussion the puppies will never learn what to say. If one puppy pins the other or if one growls and then rushes the other animal, calmly get the leash and pull the animals away from each other.

If you ever become worried about whether or not your puppy is having fun, take him out of the action for a few seconds and then let him go. If he rushes right back to play with the other dog, he was likely having fun. If he cowers, avoids the dog, or tries to leave the area, chances are good he was not having fun.

If the puppy wasn't having fun, wait a few days and try a different puppy or dog to meet. If things still aren't going well, seek the help of a professional.

Doggy Day Cares

If your puppy is a social butterfly and loves playing with other dogs, consider checking out doggy day cares and dog parks in your area.

When looking at doggy day cares, look for a facility that allows you to inspect all of the areas where your puppy would be staying. Find out how many people will be with the dogs at any time and what their level of experience is. Always ask how they would stop a dog fight and what steps they take to ensure all the dogs and puppies play well together.

If possible, find a doggy day care that has play sessions broken down by the size of dog, age, or type of play. You may not want your Maltese to play with a Great Dane if the larger dog could accidentally hurt the smaller one during play. Some dogs like to play wrestling games where they grab onto each other's snouts or necks and drag each other around. Other dogs like to play only run-and-chase games where they take turns chasing each other. You would not want to pair a puppy that only wanted to play run-and-chase with one that only wanted to wrestle.

If you are leaving your puppy at a doggy day care for several hours, find out how long he'll be out in a play group and how often he'll be in a kennel or crate. It's best to find a facility that has play sessions and nap sessions so the puppies and dogs don't get overstimulated by too much playing and get into a fight.

Make sure you ask what vaccines each animal must have to enter the facility and what cleaning protocols the owners use. Just like children at a school who pass a cold around, dogs and puppies can easily transfer parasites as well as illnesses such as kennel cough.

Not all dogs enjoy the company of other dogs. Or you may have a puppy that enjoys a few select friends but wouldn't have fun in a dog park with a bunch of strangers. Don't force your dog to go to doggy day care or to the dog park. She may have more fun at home with you.

Dog Parks

It may be best to wait until your puppy is 6 months or older and has a solid recall before you take him to a dog park. You want to make sure if you let your puppy loose to play with other dogs in a large area you have a way of catching him again.

Unlike doggy day care facilities, most dog parks don't have professional staff monitoring the doggy interactions. It's up to each owner to ensure his or her dog behaves appropriately in the dog park. Unfortunately, what one owner considers appropriate dog to dog interaction may be totally inappropriate to another owner.

One problem with dog parks is the people who come often use the facility as a social gathering spot. You often see the dog owners standing in a group drinking coffee, talking, and not paying any attention to the dogs. If two dogs get into a scuffle, there's no way to know who started it or what happened, and feelings are easily hurt—not to mention the dogs could be injured.

Always watch your puppy when she's in the dog park. If you see her getting too rough with another dog, call her away immediately or walk up to her and remove her from the situation. If your puppy is the one not having a good time and the other dog's owner won't step in, remove your puppy from the dog park. It's far better to cut playtime short than to risk her becoming scared of other dogs.

As with doggy day care facilities, check that the dog park you frequent has a means of ensuring the dogs using the park have the appropriate shots.

If you have a dog that doesn't do well sharing toys or sticks, be extremely careful at the dog park. While many parks have rules that you can't have food in the park, most allow toys. Even if the park doesn't allow toys, there are bound to be sticks on the ground. If one park visitor is throwing a ball for her dog to catch and your dog constantly rushes in to get the ball instead, be polite and move your dog to another part of the park. If your dog growls or rushes at dogs that have toys, proceed with caution in the dog park.

Dogs in a park are also expected to be social around people. If your dog is fearful of strangers, be careful in a dog park, as most dog owners will reach down and pet any dog that comes near them. If your dog jumps on everyone he meets, also consider whether he's an appropriate candidate for the dog park.

Puppy Tricks

One great thing about clicker training is how easy it is to teach your dog tricks. Most tricks start off as behaviors the dog offers naturally. For example, many dogs lift up a front paw. If your puppy understands that the click marks a behavior and you click and treat any time you see her lift a front paw, she soon will repeatedly lift her paw. You can then give that a cue, such as "shake."

If your puppy stretches outward and you click and treat when she stretches, you can often turn that into a bow. Many dogs roll onto their sides from the down position. If you begin to click and treat any time your puppy lies flat on her side, you can teach her to play dead (or perhaps the more politically correct "go to sleep").

Roll Over

Roll over is something some dogs do naturally, which you could capture with the clicker and treat; or you could teach your dog to roll over using a treat to lure him all the way over.

With the dog in a down position, put a treat right in front of his nose and have him bend his neck back up and toward his shoulder. Experiment to see which side of your dog appears to be most flexible, as some dogs will more easily roll onto one shoulder or the other.

Gradually bring the lure back farther over the dog's back until he drops a shoulder and starts to go onto his back. You can also mark that spot with the clicker and treat.

Keep working to get more of the dog following the treat until he rolls over; then have a big treat party and praise him mightily. Soon he will start offering the rollover behavior repeatedly and you can then attach a cue to it.

Weaving

You can easily teach your dog to weave through your legs as you walk using your targeting skills.

1. Stand with your legs slightly apart and ask your puppy to target your hand in front of your legs; click and treat.

2. Move your hand behind your body and ask your puppy to come through your legs to target your hand; click and treat.

3. Move a hand to the side of your body so the puppy targets back to your front; repeat the sequence for the other leg.

4. Once the puppy is reliably circling through your legs, take a step forward, and as you step forward target your puppy to walk under your leg. Soon she can be taught to weave in and out as you walk.

Some of the best tricks are just attaching funny words to things your dog does naturally. One of the greatest tricks of all time is to teach your dog to "vacuum." Just show your dog a small handful of treats, throw them on the floor, and yell, "vacuum." It is amazing how many people will congratulate you and ask how long it took you to train that trick.

What Next? Sports, Certifications, and More

If you have a puppy who enjoys learning new things, there is no limit to what you could do. There are dozens of dog sports. If you want to give back to your community, there are often opportunities in Therapy Dog work or in search and rescue. Popular dog sports are agility, dock diving, Flyball, K9 Nose Work, and rally. For the more ambitious, there is disc dog, Schutzhund (also known as IPO), competitive obedience, therapy dog work, or search and rescue. There are sports for specific types of dogs such as lure coursing, which mainly attracts sight hounds such as Whippets or Greyhounds, but is popular with any breed that will chase a small, fast-moving, furry object. There are terrier races and barn hunts, which are designed for the breeds that are supposed to chase vermin into a hole.

The Canine Good Citizen® Title

The first step for almost any more advanced endeavor is getting a Canine Good Citizen® title. This is a title offered through the American Kennel Club, but other countries have similar designations. It's a test to prove that your dog can safely be in public and that you have some type of control over her. Any dog, regardless of breed, can take the CGC® test. It doesn't matter how old your dog is when the test is administered, although the AKC encourages people to have their dogs tested when they are adults rather than puppies since temperament can change as the puppy grows up.

To pass a CGC® test, your dog needs to be able to let a stranger pet her, pick up her paws, and examine her ears. You will have to prove you have control over your puppy by having her sit, down, stay, and come as well as walk on a loose leash through a crowd of people. You'll need to show your puppy can be polite to others in public by walking her up to another person and showing she will not jump up on that person.

Part of the test also requires that you walk your dog past another dog and person, stop near the other dog and person, and show that your dog will not go to greet the other dog. There's also a three-minute separation test to see what happens if you leave your dog alone in a room with a stranger. The AKC website details the test and offers a link to find certified testers in specific geographic locations.

Meeting with Other Dog Owners

If you enjoy learning and working with your dog, consider putting together your own dog lover's group. Get together with fellow dog enthusiasts for walks in the park, dog events, training exercises, etc. It's a fun way to meet with like-minded individuals without being competitive.

If you want to be serious about a dog sport, search and rescue, or therapy dog work, it often helps to find someone who already knows the ropes to mentor you. Generally, you want to start without a dog so you can see what's required, what types of dogs do best in it, and then research what type of puppy will both best fit your lifestyle and excel at what you want to do.

Chapter 13

On the Move

- Making plans and packing for long trips with your puppy
- Keeping your traveling companion happy and healthy on the road
- Pet sitting and boarding options for times when your puppy must stay behind

Adding a puppy to your life brings much joy and happiness. It also brings a few complications, such as when you plan a trip or a vacation. With some planning and research, you can make sure that travel plans work for both you and your new family member.

Be sure to add extra time to your travel plans. Your puppy will need some time for elimination walks, some playtime to wear him out, and extra time for meals. When planning your itinerary, look for dog-friendly parks and places to do a little hiking and exploring.

When you pack, keep puppy meals, poop bags, and paper towels to wipe up any messes all handy. Some chew items, treats, and fresh water should also be easily accessible. Do your best to plan how much food you will need for the trip. Some premium brands may not be available where you are traveling.

At stops, get the puppy out for a quick walk before you take a break. Once both of you are comfortable, consider a longer walk or some playtime. You won't be able to totally tire your puppy out, but if you take the edge off he will be much happier about returning to the car and his crate. Be sure to give him a treat when he is put back in the crate.

As tempting as it may be to let your pup really run, keep him on lead at parks and rest areas. Stray dogs, speeding cars, and toxic litter are just some of the temptations that could lure your puppy and lead to injury or illness.

It helps to have a copy of your pup's most recent vaccinations and any veterinary care with you. Sticking a copy in the glove compartment after each veterinary clinic visit means you will have up-to-date health information with you at all times.

Traveling with Your Puppy

Packing for a Puppy

It is very important that you organize ahead of time when traveling with a puppy. You need to pack for the puppy's needs as well as remember your own clothes, medications, etc. Essentials for taking your puppy on a trip include

- A crate for safe travel and confinement in a hotel or a guest room at a friend's house
- A supply of your puppy's food
- A leash and collar or harness
- Identification tags for the collar or harness and a copy of the microchip number for your wallet
- Water and food bowls
- A copy of your puppy's vaccination certificate and any other pertinent health information
- Toys and treats for when you take breaks
- A first-aid kit
- Chew items for quiet times
- A soft blanket or mat for bedding

Practicing Car Travel

Your puppy may need some practice to become a good traveler. Try to take the pup out for some short drives to a pleasant place. Drive to a local ice cream stand for a treat. Plan a drive to a nice park and take a long hike. You want your puppy to associate the car with positive things—not just visits to the veterinary clinic.

Dealing with Car Sickness

Some puppies have a tendency to get carsick. Ginger capsules can help, or ask your veterinarian for some medication. Many puppies do just fine if the car is cool and they have fresh air. Keep the air conditioning on if possible. Use a crate fan if needed.

Try to avoid routes with lots of turns, potholes, and frequent stops. Highway travel is best from the point of view of a nauseated pup. Some puppies ride better if they can see out of their crate, while others do best in a quiet, dark corner of the car. Experiment to see what works best for your puppy.

Plan Mealtimes

If your puppy gets carsick, you may need to put some extra care into mealtime planning. Start early so he can eat at least an hour before you head out in the car. That also gives your pup plenty of time to eat and then enjoy a long walk and eliminate. This does mean extra time on a noon break as well. Assume your puppy will need to stretch his legs every 100 miles or so. Provide fresh water on each stop in addition to leaving a bowl with ice cubes carefully fastened in the crate, so he can lick some water as needed.

Sticking to Routines

It gets tricky when traveling to stick to your puppy's regular routine. This is especially true if you are traveling across time zones. As much as possible, try to stick to your pup's normal times for getting up, eating, walking, naps, and bedtime. This will help to keep his housetraining on schedule. Think of your puppy as a toddler who does best with a regular routine.

Your first aid kit should include something for an upset stomach or diarrhea, eye wash or artificial tears to flush eyes and wounds, a rectal thermometer, gauze for a bandage or emergency muzzle, antihistamine, and antibiotic ointment. You may want some other items as well, but these are essential.

Staying in Hotels

While on the road, you can find many pet-friendly hotel chains. To be safe, call ahead to be sure an individual facility welcomes pets. Some places have restrictions on the size or number of pets allowed at one time. Don't try to sneak your puppy into a non-pet-friendly room.

Your puppy should never be left alone in a hotel room. He may bark, chew on furniture, or have an accident on the carpet. If you act irresponsibly, you may ruin hotel policy for other pet owners. At night, have your pup sleep in his beloved crate. Tuck him in with an extra chew if he needs one. Always clean up after your puppy and deposit his poop bags in outdoor trash containers.

Most campgrounds also allow pets but do have restrictions, such as always keeping the pets on lead or confined. This is for your puppy's welfare as well as for the comfort of other campers.

Staying as a Guest in a Home

All of the rules about courtesy apply when you are staying at the home of a friend or relative—maybe even more so. Make sure your puppy is properly introduced to any resident animals, or simply keep them separate. Always supervise when toys are down for the dogs to play with or treats are handed out.

Be sure you follow the "house rules" where you stay. If your puppy is used to getting on the couch at night, but they have a strict rule of no pets on the furniture, your pup will have to abide by their rule.

Don't trust a safely fenced-in yard until you have walked the perimeter yourself. Fencing that's safe for the resident Labrador Retriever may not be safe for your terrier puppy. You don't want your pup chewing on toxic plants or digging up a valuable rosebush. Better still, take your puppy out on a leash so you can easily clean up after him and keep track of his elimination times.

Never leave your puppy loose alone with new animals or unknown children. It is better to be safe than sorry. A tired pup in a strange place may not behave with his usual good spirits.

Public Recreation Areas

Many beaches have strict rules about pets. They may only allow dogs at certain times of day. They may restrict dogs to on-leash only. Some beaches totally ban pets due to nesting waterfowl. Other beaches allow dogs, but not in the water. While it may be disappointing, you need to respect these rules. Fines are heavy and may be accompanied by being banned from the area.

Many national parks, state parks, and state forests do allow dogs. Generally they are required to be on lead and you must have proof of a current rabies vaccination with you. The rules are to keep your puppy safe from wildlife such as coyotes, skunks, and porcupines, and also to keep wildlife such as fawns safe from your puppy.

While hiking, remember to bring water for your pup to drink and a snack or two. Even pristine-looking lakes may harbor parasites like giardia. Don't expect your puppy to wear a backpack and carry supplies until he is close to 1 year of age. Even then, it should be very lightweight. Keep in mind your pup's age and stamina when planning a hike. You really don't want to have to carry him all the way back to the trailhead!

Tourist Attractions

Some of the better-known tourist attractions provide kennels on site for free or for rent. Your puppy can safely stay in a run with water and a watchful attendant while your family enjoys rides and exhibits. Never plan on simply leaving your pup in the car. Cars heat up rapidly, and while your car may have been in the shade when you left, the sun will move while you're away. You don't want a day of fun to end with a sick or dying puppy due to hyperthermia.

Traveling Without Your Puppy

There are times when it truly is best to leave your puppy behind. Some trips simply aren't puppy friendly, and your pet will be happier and safer if left at home or boarded in a kennel.

Flying

Any trip that requires flying is a trip to consider leaving your pup at home. Small puppies might be able to fit in a carrier under the seat. Most airlines have quotas for how many pets they allow in the cabin on certain flights, and some don't allow pets in the cabin at all. While many dogs fly in the cargo hold with no problem, there are very few good reasons to fly with your puppy.

Hanging at Home

If a family member lives nearby or is not going on the trip, you may have a built-in pet sitter. If your situation is uncomplicated—a puppy-proof fenced area for him to eliminate in and get some exercise, and a healthy pup who requires the minimum of care—this is perfect. Be sure to write out your pup's daily routine carefully and thoroughly, and double-check it a day or so later to be sure you didn't leave anything out. Set firm rules about only walking on a leash, and be clear about house rules, such as whether the puppy is allowed on furniture. Carefully outline feeding times and amounts.

If you live in a high-rise apartment and your closest relative is a senior citizen who uses a walker, rethink the family member plan. Even young, healthy relatives may balk at having to take a puppy downstairs to walk outside in all kinds of weather multiple times a day. Ideally you don't want your pup's housetraining to backslide.

Neighbors and Friends

You may also want to look for a neighbor or friend who might love to stay at your house and enjoy a "part-time puppy." Think of the friend whose spouse has dog allergies so they can't have a dog of their own. Or the responsible teenager next door who would love to have a dog but can't. Do your unofficial background checks thoroughly to be sure the person involved understands and is willing to put in the extra time a puppy requires. Patience and a sense of humor, as well as willingness to follow your directives, are big pluses.

A Pet Sitter

An excellent solution for your puppy's care can be to arrange for a pet sitter. Organizations such as Pet Sitters International provide trained and bonded animal caretakers. These people can come to your house as many times a day as you need them to care for your puppy. This is not a place to skimp. Be prepared to cover the cost for extra visits if your pup will need frequent meals and outings.

An experienced pet sitter will guide you to fill out detailed directions for the proper care of your puppy. Double-check to be sure you have covered everything! Consider making a recording of yourself reading a fairly dry book—no exciting thrillers—to be played for your pup when he will be left alone. That may help him slip off into a quiet nap in his crate.

Other Possible Pet Sitters

There are other possible options for experienced and trustworthy pet sitters. If your puppy attends day care or a training class, you might want to ask an assistant who works there. Often veterinary technicians are willing to house sit for a client's puppy. These people have the advantage of having met your puppy ahead of time, which is helpful.

Boarding Kennels

A reputable, well-cared-for boarding kennel is another excellent option for your pup. Ask friends and knowledgeable dog people like your puppy class instructor for recommendations. Your veterinarian may do some boarding or may have facilities to recommend as well.

Always visit a potential boarding kennel ahead of time. Call ahead to find out when morning cleanup is done so you don't arrive in the middle of the kennel's busiest time. You want to be able to check out the runs and cages as well as have some time speaking to both the kennel staff and the manager.

Kennel Requirements

Some kennels will ask you to provide your own food for your puppy, especially if he eats an unusual premium food. Be sure his food is clearly labeled with both his name and the amounts to feed. The boarding kennel may not be able to keep to his usual routine, but they will try to accommodate a puppy's schedule as best they can.

Boarding kennels also have certain health requirements. This is for the safety of your own pup and all of the other dogs at the kennel. Find out any required vaccinations ahead of time so your puppy can be fully protected.

Different kennels will have different rules about bringing toys and bedding for your puppy. Knowing how puppies chew, they may prefer their own sturdy mats. Don't be upset if you leave a toy or bed and your pup decides to destroy them just for fun.

Extras at the Kennel

Many kennels will offer extras if you want them for your puppy. It is worth it to pay for some extra exercise and play time. A tired pup is a good pup! Some extra walking time may help keep his housetraining schedule on track as well. It is also wise to schedule a bath for your puppy on your day of pickup. Despite the best efforts of the kennel, many puppies manage to get dirty or pick up some odors. A last-minute bath will mean a clean, sweet-smelling pup in your arms.

Emergency Plans

Whether your puppy stays at home with a devoted neighbor or enjoys his visit at a kennel, you need to make arrangements for any emergencies. Be sure you leave all emergency contact information clearly in sight at home or on a form at the kennel. If you have a nearby friend or neighbor who could be contacted, include their contact information as well as your own—especially if you will be far away. Make sure they are authorized to approve care. That person may need to make a quick judgment if your pup needs emergency surgery or care. Make sure they know your wishes.

Have your regular veterinarian's information available as well as the emergency service you plan to use if your veterinary clinic does not provide coverage 24/7. It is a good idea to leave your credit card information for the pet sitter or with your veterinarian to cover costs if you can't be reached immediately for an emergency. You can always set a maximum amount for immediate care, but that way your pup is covered in case you are on a plane or otherwise unreachable.

Appendix A
Glossary

bacterin   A vaccination against a bacterial disease.

Be a Tree   A program from Doggone Safe that teaches children how to safely interact with dogs by standing completely still and ignoring the dog.

behavior   Your dog's actions and patterns of actions. Behaviors can be influenced by rewards so the puppy continues to offer them if desired.

breed restrictions   Some apartments, towns, and even insurance firms have restrictions on what dog breeds are allowed.

Canine Good Citizen®   This is an American Kennel Club program to acknowledge and promote responsible dog ownership and well-behaved dogs. The CGC is often the first step into any dog sport or therapy work.

clicker   Used in marker training, this is generally a plastic object that will make a noise when a button is pushed.

congenital   Present at birth; generally refers to defects. They may or may not be genetic in origin.

crate   Generally made of wire or plastic, the crate is an awesome place to park your puppy when he or she can't be underfoot.

deciduous teeth   Baby teeth—a puppy's first set of teeth, which are replaced by "adult teeth" by about 8 to 10 months of age.

dominance   Dogs competing for resources such as food or shelter may exert dominance over each other to see which one gets the resource. Your puppy is not dominating you. This is a much-misused term in dog training.

hand targeting   Teaching the puppy to touch a hand. This can help him learn to do many other behaviors.

housetraining The process of teaching a puppy where to relieve himself; it could be outside or in a specifically designated spot.

lure This is something the dog likes—usually a food treat or toy—used to help him assume a position or do something you want him to do.

mange Skin problems caused by mite infestations.

mark In training, this is the process of acknowledging a behavior immediately after it happens.

MDR 1 Multi Drug Resistance 1, a genetic mutation that interferes with the metabolism of certain drugs; most common in herding breeds and herding breed mixes.

microchip An integrated circuit, about the size of a grain of rice, implanted under an animal's skin. Its unique identifying numbers can be read by a scanner and help reunite a lost pet with its owner.

murmur An unusual heart sound caused by turbulence in the blood flow.

negative punishment When something rewarding is removed or taken away. This is a useful training tool for puppies.

negative reinforcement Something the dog dislikes is used during unwanted behavior and then is removed when the dog's behavior changes. This is not recommended in training.

no-pull harness Many firms make special harnesses that will discourage a puppy from pulling. This can be an excellent way to take a puppy for a walk.

OFA or Orthopedic Foundation for Animals The primary group keeping track of genetic health screenings for dogs. Initially hip dysplasia was the only disease tracked, but now many inherited problems are looked at—both orthopedic ones and other inherited defects.

patella Kneecap; part of the stifle joint in the rear leg.

positive punishment When something the dog dislikes is used to decrease the frequency of a behavior. This is not recommended for training your puppy.

positive reinforcement The process of adding something good to the dog's training as rewards for cooperation or behavior. This is a highly effective way to train.

praise The process of using a happy tone of voice to mark and reward good behavior.

reward Something the dog likes; it can be praise, treats, toys, or petting, and is used to acknowledge good behavior.

socialization This is the process of introducing a puppy to the world around him. The more proper socialization at an early age, the more well-adjusted your puppy will be.

titer A blood sample used to detect immunity against a disease.

treats Anything the dog really enjoys eating. Treats make an excellent reward.

zoonotic or zoonoses Diseases that can pass from animals to people and vice versa.

Appendix B
Resources

Behavior

American Veterinary Society of Animal Behavior, Position Statements and Handouts, http://avsabonline.org/resources/position-statements

Don't Shoot the Dog!: The New Art of Teaching and Training, by Karen Pryor, 2002, Ringpress Books

Fired Up, Frantic, and Freaked Out: Training the Crazy Dog from Over the Top to Under Control, by Laura VanArendonk Baugh, 2013, Aeclipse Press.

Help for Your Fearful Dog: A Step-by-Step Guide to Helping Your Dog Conquer His Fears, by Nicole Wilde, 2006, Phantom Publishing

I'll be Home Soon: How to Prevent and Treat Separation Anxiety, by Patricia McConnell, 2000, McConnell Publishing

Virtual Behaviorist, a website run by the ASPCA, www.aspca.org

Whole Dog Journal, either print or online edition, www.wholedogjournal.com

Children and Dogs

Dog Gone Safe, http://www.doggonesafe.com, Dog bite prevention through education, offers the Be a Tree program to help children safely learn to interact with dogs.

Living with Kids and Dogs .. Without Losing Your Mind, 2nd Edition, by Colleen Pelar, 2013, Dream Dog Productions

Clicker Training

Getting Started: Clicker Training for Dogs, by Karen Pryor, 2005, Sunshine Books

Karen Pryor Clicker Training, www.clickertraining.com

Feeding

Association of American Feed Control Officials: http://www.aafco.org/

Balance IT: https://secure.balanceit.com/

Grooming

International Professional Groomers: http://www.ipgicmg.com/

International Society of Canine Cosmetologists: https://www.facebook.com/isccpetstylists

National Dog Groomers Association of America: http://www.nationaldoggroomers.com/

Medical

American Animal Hospital Association: http://www.aaha.org/pet_owner/

American Heartworm Society: http://www.heartwormsociety.org/

American Veterinary Medical Association: https://www.avma.org/Pages/home.aspx

ASPCA Animal Poison Control: http://www.aspca.org/pet-care/animal-poison-control

Companion Animal Parasite Council: http://www.capcvet.org/

Orthopedic Foundation for Animals: http://www.offa.org/

Pet Poison Hotline: http://www.petpoisonhelpline.com/poisons/

Pet Sitting

Pet Sitters International: https://www.petsit.com/

Finding a Dog Trainer

Association of Professional Dog Trainers offers a way to search for trainers by geographic region: https://www.apdt.com/petowners/ts/

Karen Pryor Academy, find trainers who graduated from KPA: https://www.karenpryoracademy.com/find-a-trainer

breeders, 15

bringing puppies home, 41
  adjustment time, 42
  bonding, 54–55
  first night, 52–53
  kids, 56–57
  meeting
    family members, 50–51
    other pets, 44–49

brushes, 122

brushing, 126–127

budgets, 20–21

C

C/T (click and treat), 87

Canine Good Citizen title, 278

canned foods, 62–63

car rides, 210–213, 283

car sickness, 283

cats, 38, 48

chamois towels, 123

chasing moving things, 256–257

chest examinations, 146

chewing, 242–243

choke chains, 31

choking, 180

choosing puppies, 3
  breeds, 5
  costs, 6
  fenced yards, 6
  grooming needs, 7
  home evaluations, 8–9
  kid considerations, 4, 11
  litter observations, 11
  meeting the puppy, 12–13
  part of the family, 5
  right age to bring home, 10
  size, 5
  socialization, 7

city life *versus* country life, 176

clicker training, 190–195
  crates, 87
  exercises, 192–195
  getting started, 191
  resources, 293

clothing, 23

coccidia, 160

collars, 30–31

combs, 127

come cue, 222–225

Companion Animal Parasite
  Council website, 293

conditioners, 128

core vaccines, 148

country *versus* city life, 176

CPR, 179

crate training, 77
  choosing crates, 78
  clickers, 87
  contents, 80
  creative times, 86
  going in, 82–85
  housetraining, 79
  placement, 81
  punishment, 79
  rewards, 87
  troubleshooting, 87
  upset behaviors, 86

crates, 28
  choosing, 78
  contents, 80
  placement, 81

cues, 196–197

curved scissors, 123

D

demodectic mites, 162

dental care, 156–157

dewclaws, 125

diarrhea, 180

digging, 240–241

dog blow dryers, 123

dog parks, 275

Doggone Safe website, 37, 292

doggy day cares, 274

double-coated brushing, 126

down cue, 218–221

dry foods, 60–61

drying coats, 129

E

ear care, 130–131

elbow dysplasia, 174

electric collars, 31

electrical shocks, 179

emergency clinics, 143

enjoying socialization, 106

existing pets
  introducing, 44–49
  preparations, 38–39

external parasites, 162–165

eye care, 132–133

F

family member
  introductions, 50–51

FDA natural foods definition, 66

fears, 103, 106

fences, 6, 9

fetch, 264–265

finicky eaters, 61

first aid kits, 283

first night, 52–53

fleas, 164

medium-coated brushing, 126

metal combs, 122

microchips, 182

mites, 162–163

mitts, 123

murmurs, 166

N

nail trimming, 124–125

National Dog Groomers Association of America website, 293

natural foods, 66–67

negative punishment, 187

negative reinforcement, 187

neutering, 152–155

new socialization places, 112–113

nipping, 244–245

no pull harnesses, 32

non-core vaccines, 149

O

OCD (Osteochondritis Dissecans), 175

older dog preparations, 39

on and off cues, 214–215

organic foods, 67

Orthopedic Foundation for Animals, 169, 293

orthopedic problems
large dogs, 172–175
small dogs, 168–170

other dogs
introducing, 44–47
meeting on walks, 119, 207
preparations, 39

owner groups, 278

P

packing for traveling, 282

panosteitis, 175

park socialization, 116–117

PDA (Patent Ductus Arteriosus), 167

people food, 74

pet health insurance, 183

Pet Poison Hotline, 181, 293

pet sitters, 287, 293

pet stores, 16

petting dogs on heads, 105

physical examinations, 146–147

pin brushes, 122

plastic kennels, 78

play dates, 272–275

playground socialization, 116–117

poisonings, 181

positive punishment, 187

positive reinforcement, 187

positive training, 190–195

potty pads, 94

power cords, 23

preservatives, 67

prong collars, 31

protein sources, 63

Pryor, Karen websites, 293

public recreation areas, 284–285

pulling, 205

punishments
crates, 79
versus rewards, 186

puppy mills, 16

puppy proofing
houses, 22–24
yards, 26–27

Q–R

raw/home-cooked foods, 64–65

rescue groups, 14

resource guarding, 252–255

retained teeth, 157

retained testicles, 154

retractable leashes, 33

rewards
crate training, 87
identifying, 188–189
versus punishments, 186
toys as, 189
treats. See treats

roll over, 276

rope circle game, 269

rotary grinding tools, 123

roundworms, 158

rugs/flooring, 24

S

sarcoptic mites, 163

scary objects, 106

scissor-type nail cutters, 123

seat belt harnesses, 32

seizures, 141, 181

shampoos, 128

short-coated brushing, 126

signs of stress, 100–102

sit cue, 216–217

skunk odor removal, 129

slicker brushes, 122

slickers, 127

small animal pets, 39, 49

small dog orthopedic problems, 168–170

soft cloths, 122

soft-bristle brushes, 122

spaying, 152–155

sport harnesses, 32

sports, 278

stairs, 115

stay cue, 222–225

staying home alone training, 202–203

stenosis defects, 167

stepping onto a mat exercise, 194–195

sticky item removal, 127

stool problems, 140

stress, 100–103

supplements, 64

T

table food, 74

tapeworms, 159

tear stains, 133

teeth, 156–157

thining shears, 123

ticks, 165

toothbrushes/toothpaste, 123

tourist attractions, 285

toys
  buying, 34
  food-dispensing, 30
  puppy proofing, 23
  as rewards, 189

trainers, 228–229, 293

training classes, 228–229

trash containers, 24

traveling, 281
  car sickness, 283
  first aid kits, 283
  flying, 286
  hotel stays, 284
  house guest, 284
  mealtimes, 283
  packing, 282
  practicing, 283
  public recreation areas, 284–285
  routines, 283
  tourist attractions, 285
  without puppies, 287–289

treat bags, 189

treats, 74–75
  avoiding, 75
  finding enjoyable, 188
  food as, 74
  homemade, 75
  housetraining, 91
  ranking, 189
  table food, 74
  treat bags, 189

tricks, 276–277

trimming nails, 124–125

tug game, 260–263

U–V

vaccinations, 148–151

valve defects, 167

veterinarians, 142–143

veterinary visits
  physical examination, 146–147
  preparations, 144–145
  vaccinations, 148–151

Virtual Behaviorist website, 292

vomiting, 180

W–X–Y–Z

waiting at doors training, 198–199

walking, 204–209
  floor surfaces, 114
  heel, 208–209
  let's go cue, 206
  meeting strangers/other dogs, 119, 207
  pulling, 205
  stairs, 115

washing, 128–129

water, 30, 72–73

weaving, 277

whipworms, 160

Whole Dog Journal website, 292

wire crates, 78

yards
  digging, 240–241
  fences, 6–9
  puppy proofing, 26–27

All photos by Katherine Scheele, © Dorling Kindersley, with the following exceptions: page 24: Melissa Duffy © Dorling Kindersley; page 38: Tracy Morgan Animal Photography © Dorling Kindersley; page 39 (bottom): Dave King © Dorling Kindersley; page 49: Steve Teague © Dorling Kindersley; page 67: Tracy Morgan © Dorling Kindersley; page 123 (bottom left): Gerard Brown © Dorling Kindersley; page 163: Connie Swaim © Dorling Kindersley; page 182: Tracy Morgan © Dorling Kindersley; pages 252–253: Jane Burton © Dorling Kindersley.